THE
BODINE
Story

THE BODINE

Story

❧

From Chicken Coop to Industry Leader

by

DAVID YAWN

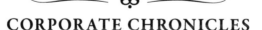

CORPORATE CHRONICLES
A Lighthouse Leadership Imprint
David Yawn Communications

First American Edition
ISBN 978-0-615-32722-8

Corporate Chronicles
A Lighthouse Memoirs Imprint
David Yawn Communications
1082 Kings Park Road
Memphis 38117

Designed by BrianGroppe Design

Contents

ABOUT THE AUTHOR

Author David McDonald Yawn has spent a career of three decades in professional business writing and editing. He has edited nine published book manuscripts. After working in editorial capacities at *Memphis Business Journal*, FedEx, International Paper, Baker Donelson law firm and *The Daily News*, he is now engaged in full-time independent contract assignments.

This is dedicated to my two wives.
In loving memory of
Virginia (Jinnie) Shannon Bodine,
without whom the company
and the school would never have happened,
and in deep appreciation to
Peggy Jemison Bodine
without whom this story
would not have been told.

—Dick Bodine

⚜

Introduction

From Chicken Coop to Industry Leader

Dick Bodine relaxes in a comfortable computer chair in his Memphis high-rise condo and manipulates a joystick to bank his simulated airplane through a cluster of clouds and then onward over a coastline.

His physical presence is far removed from his years at the helm of his namesake Bodine Company which he founded alongside his wife and business partner, Virginia, known by all as "Jinnie." However, his thoughts are never far from the business he started out of a chicken coop and that grew to the point when many years later, it drew the attraction and ultimately, ownership purchase by a top multi-national company.

This engineering school graduate capitalized on his passion and abilities to tinker, which enabled him to develop new products the market never knew it needed until he devised them. Dick was never satisfied with turning out conventional products, but was always the master craftsman of electronics, intrigued to this very day with new computer gadgets, GPS systems and computer programs. These abiding interests have served him well, and he and Jinnie also served their communities well. They were not satisfied to build their little empire within corporate America, rather they and their employees gave back time and again.

One of their most enduring legacies, in addition to the vibrant company they founded, is The Bodine School, which they established through the inspiration of their son's much-too-brief life and his own learning needs. The Memphis school meets a very real need for excellent training of children with learning disabilities. It is now in its fourth decade and is fully accredited.

In 1988 as they retired, Dick and Jinnie sold the company in its entirety to their employees – an almost unparalleled practice. They did this by making the buyout possible through financing the sale themselves with the provision that it be paid off in 15 years. They then retired to St. Croix, Virgin Islands, where they enjoyed the beautiful island and built a home on what they considered the prettiest site in the Caribbean.

"You need to have dreams and goals but always be thankful for what you have, and during hard times, remember the good times and in good times, remember the hard times." —Al Lyons

Jinnie Bodine died of cancer in 1999, and sometime later, Dick married fellow Memphian Peggy Boyce Jemison, who also had lost her longtime mate, Frank Jemison.

The parts of the year when Dick and Peggy were not living on St. Croix, they have enjoyed visiting Memphis to reconnect with friends, family and current and former Bodine Co. employees. Most recently, they moved back to their hometown of Memphis as their permanent residence.

During these past intervals in Tennessee, they were able to attend grandchildren's graduations and weddings and outings such as the city's annual barbecue cooking contest, for which the Bodine Co. unfalteringly wins trophies that now festoon the company dining room.

The Bodine Company continues to design and manufacture emergency and specialty lighting solutions for today's and tomorrow's lighting industry. It has become a hallmark of quality, reliability, code compliance and American ingenuity through the creation of products for a variety of applications. These applications include fluorescent, HID metal halide, LED and generator-supplied lighting. Products are sold through a network of manufacturers' representatives and electrical distributors for field installation or directly to lighting fixture manufacturers for factory installation.

The Bodines leave a legacy as accomplished business people and as generous contributors to their communities. This story demonstrates that a business can succeed and still have a heart and can treat its employees in a manner designed for all to benefit. This account additionally relates how a company can give part of its revenues back to the community and still make a profit.

The Bodine Co. has since grown to such a stature that it attracted the attention of Philips Electronics in the Netherlands, which acquired it in 2007 to broaden the worldwide electronics company's reach and product lines. The current owners continue the tradition of community involvement through support of civic and educational programs in the Memphis area.

This spirit is perhaps epitomized in the words of a Christmas letter penned in 2004 by former Bodine president, Al Lyons, to company employees: "You need to have dreams and goals but always be thankful for what you have, and during hard times, remember the good times and in good times, remember the hard times."

This book will attempt to portray the life work of Dick Bodine, who, with Jinnie, built the company and founded the Bodine School. It will trace the history of the Bodines to show their generous entrepreneurship. In doing so, this book will tell the story not only of the building of a successful company, but also of the making of a generous man.

THE BODINE STORY

I

The Making of the Man: Childhood, the War and the Family Business

RICHARD HILL BODINE, KNOWN AS DICK, WAS born in 1924. In the city at large, Mayor Rowlett Paine's administration was spurring city planning and downtown experienced a building boom. The streetcar system contributed to the early growth rings in Memphis with downtown as the main connecting point. Downtown Memphis was the unparalleled nexus of retail, hotels, entertainment, the court system, and business in general. It was home of retail establishments like Woolworth's, Kress, Lowensteins, Gerber's, Goldsmiths and Bry's. The widespread introduction of the automobile pushed that envelope out further, with auto registrations increasing from 19,000 in 1920 to 42,000 by the time Dick turned a year old. Enough development was occurring that Memphis introduced its first zoning laws between 1920 and 1922, serving to protect property values.

When Dick was just three, the Memphis riverfront would be inundated by flood waters from the Mississippi Valley Flood of 1927. This was a time when the levee system was not a force strong enough to contend with the rising waters of this major artery. It marked the greatest flood of the Mississippi River on record to that point. Physically, Memphis itself wasn't impinged, but it became a headquarters for relief operations in the Mid-South. The city of some 250,000 citizens and 286 businesses would show it was a survivor, indeed. It was a city which had experienced the Yellow Fever epidemics of the turn of the century and had sent its sons to the battlefronts in the Great War of the teens. Yet one of its greatest economic challenges would confront both the city and the nation some three years later with the Great Depression.

This was the decade of the erection of The Peabody Hotel and the Sterick Building downtown. Major employers during this time included Memphis Packing Co. (later Armour), E.L Bruce Hardwood Flooring, Fisher Body Works, Buckeye, Piggly Wiggly and Federal Compress. Sears Roebuck & Co. opened its mammoth retail and catalog store in the Crosstown area in 1927. A few years later, the city completed its municipal airport. Nationwide, this was the era of the popular emergence of Charles Lindberg, Babe Ruth, Al Jolson and William Faulkner.

Dick grew up in a well-known and prosperous family with a strong Memphis heritage. Great-grandfather John Leonard Norton was one of the members of the original Memphi Society, which established the predecessor to the longstanding Memphis Cotton Carnival. Dick's grandfather, Cooper P. Bodine, was a banker and his father, R.H. Bodine, was a cotton and lumber executive.

Dick and his sister, Mary Budd, spent their school years and childhood in a substantial Memphis home in Chickasaw Gardens. After graduation from 8th grade at Teachers Training Junior High School, Dick went away to the Baylor School, a preparatory academy in Chattanooga. At Baylor, he played tennis and soccer.

This was a break from his boyhood buddy, Everett Norfleet, who went to Culver Military School. Everett and Dick were like brothers. Both liked to tinker with electronics as kids. During the summers, they often spent the night at one or the other's

Dick as young man.

Dick's sister, Mary Budd Bodine.

homes and both were subject to parental discipline, regardless of which house they were visiting.

"Everett's mother didn't like the bats that flew around her patio at night, which gave us a chance to earn some money," Dick recalled. "We made a deal with her. We would shoot them for a quarter apiece while she was out for the evening. We got Everett's .410-gauge shotgun and shot up a whole box of shells and managed to get just one bat. Financially, we were not coming out very well, so we were anxious to keep it to show her. We decided to put it in her refrigerator. When she found the bat there, we really caught the mischief for it."

Any punishment one boy received, the other got too, because both sets of parents treated them like brothers. When Dick was at Baylor, Everett was attending Culver. Everett later became a builder of homes and warehouses, forming Bell & Norfleet.

Both also shared ham radio operating as hobbies. Dick and Everett enjoyed taking equipment apart and putting it back together. In each of their homes, the boys established their "shops" in the basements so they could work better with radio sets and various related electrical parts and equipment.

As teenagers, they built a gadget that used a pen to record dots and dashes of Morse Code onto paper that would move past the pen to record the code. As they fiddled with other projects and tried out a lot of devices, some worked and others didn't. It was all part of the trial-and-error learning process that Dick would carry with him into adult life. Later, Bodine Co. workers would describe something faintly similar to this approach as the Bodine Way. At Bodine, it meant a method of designing something to make it work, and then removing as many parts as possible to see if the device would still function. The two friends also often tested many of their devices on Everett's younger brother, Dunbar Abston, who was a pretty good sport about the "surprises."

When Dick was 16 and 17 years old, he worked at Buckeye Cellulose (now Buckeye Technologies) during the summers as an electrician's helper. This further honed his hobby-craft to varying early degrees. "My duties were primarily as a gopher to get whatever the electricians might need," Dick recalled. "I did learn to rewind large electrical motors and do some other jobs in the shop. That was where I got my very first paycheck."

In 1942, World War II was under way and at the age of 18, Dick went off to Georgia Tech where he spent a semester. Soon afterward, the college had some Army recruiters come to campus and tell Dick, "If you join the Reserves, you can stay in school until you graduate."

However, that was not the way it worked. He signed up and two months later, was called up. He would remain in the Army Infantry until 1946, the year after the war ended.

After Dick's basic training, he was assigned to Ft. Leonard Wood in Missouri, then to Ft. Benning, Ga., where he was designated under the Signal Corps umbrella after undergoing testing. There, he spent three months in radio school.

The World War II infantryman from Memphis then qualified and was invited to participate in a specialized initiative known as the Army Specialized Training Program, or ASTP. It was an assignment designed to let those who qualified return to college. This training lasted from the summer of 1943 until the spring of 1944, primarily at Colorado State College, now Colorado State University, in Ft. Collins. Life there, as chronicled in a book by former Army buddy, Jack Rhodes Daunder, called "Dear Mom and Dad," took on some of the same atmosphere of any university campus, although students were always reminded by their superiors that they were under military jurisdiction.

Jack chronicled it this way in his book: "I found that life became a matter of the right way, the wrong way and the Army way. To survive, you did it the Army way. Military justice was based on 'the book' and it constantly hung over your head. It was always a threat which was held over military personnel if they got out of line. Leadership too often was based on how many stripes or what bar you had on your shoulder and the constant threat of the worst work details, denial of passes or a court martial."

Jack also writes about lighthearted times with Dick and their going to the movies, playing pool, football, basketball, getting into some boxing and wrestling matches and enjoying photography. It wasn't uncommon for them to take pictures at sorority dances.

His buddy also writes about how Dick scored second-highest in his group in advanced electrical engineering tests. The two would trade off helping each other with Dick excelling in physics and Jack in history. That program also would send Dick to Lincoln, Nebraska, which would play a pivotal role in the next part of his life. The Army subsequently closed the ASTP program because it needed men for the war effort. When the Army closed the ASTP program, it put men with demonstrated high IQs into the Army.

Even more momentous was Dick's meeting his future wife, Virginia "Jinnie" Shannon in her hometown of Lincoln during the brief ASTP special assignment. They introduced themselves to each other during a ping pong table game at a USO where she was volunteering. Many years later, the two would often be seen during breaks playing a spirited game of ping pong at tables in the break room of the Bodine Co. The two began writing to each other after Dick left Lincoln.

"The first two or three years we knew each other, we were together just 16 days. The rest was by mail," Dick recalled. That includes Dick hitchhiking to Lincoln on a three-day pass when he was stationed in Colorado.

While Dick was in the Army, Jinnie attended Northwestern University and earned a degree in industrial engineering. She

Dick in Japan during the occupational phase immediately after WWII, taking a more leisurely moment with horseshoes.

sometimes kidded that the Engineering Department was the only place she could find boys. When she wasn't taking college classes, Jinnie also worked for Western Electric. After she was graduated, she worked as an industrial engineer for a motor scooter company.

Meanwhile, Dick was training in the 97th Infantry Division, which was preparing to invade Japan. All ASTP schools in the 7th Service Command were assigned to the 97th. With the Battle of the Bulge under way, the Army badly needed men and shipped Dick and other troops in his battalion to France on the Sea Robin, a small craft. "I was so seasick that I ate three meals in seven days," he said. "If anything happened, they would lock us down in the hold and you would hear guns go off. It was tough because you couldn't do anything while in the hold, but just sit and wait for the pounding to cease."

Dick went through Europe as a radio operator whose job it was to provide radio communication connections for a colonel. He drove a jeep installed with radios and had to keep up with the colonel and his driver in their jeep. Over a period of time, they rolled from France into Germany.

He served during the course of the war as an infantryman in both the Pacific and European theaters of conflict. Dick was a PFC (private first class) when he got out of the service. "I was a lot like the cartoon strip, Beetle Bailey. He was modeled after me," he said, laughing.

There were many wartime memories. "We were along a road in convoy blackout conditions late at night. Everyone stopped. Here comes a lieutenant walking alongside the convoy, saying, 'Get your ties out of your packs; we are in Patton's territory!' The troops had to rummage around and fish out their wrinkled ties and put them on." Dick wasn't always dressed up. Sometimes, he wore an apron in the kitchen. "I got all the KP and everything they could throw at me," he said. "I figured I knew more than they did and I didn't get along with my superiors. I was an obnoxious brat."

With the end of the Battle of the Ruhr Pocket, the 97th Infantry Division (Trident) received orders to move to the Third Army sector along the Czechoslovakian border. Its mission was to protect the left flank of Gen. Patton's spearhead, plunging southward. The motorized march was forced and the members of this division known as "Tridents" covered the 560 kilometers as rapidly as refueling and feeding the troops would permit. They arrived in the area of operations after a very cold ride in open vehicles.

The major offensive action for the 97th was the seizure of a war factory, administration and communications center in Cheb, also the site of a large airport. Intelligence reports indicated that there were about 1,300 German troops as well as a Hungarian artillery school and other units along the combat front.

On Victory in Europe (VE) Day, Dick was on a rooftop busily wiring a radio in Czechoslovakia when another soldier walked by him and gave him the news: "Bodine, don't you know the war is over?"

After the liberation of Europe, Dick was shipped out to be retrained to take part in the invasion of Japan and his battalion was engaged in amphibious landing preparations. The U.S. soon afterward dropped atomic bombs on Hiroshima and Nagasaki, leading to a Japanese surrender. He then went with American occupation forces to Japan. They were on a ship for 30 days before landing because food rations were low in the ports.

Through it all, Dick's reputation for working with electronics had gained momentum. In Japan, Dick taught GIs electronics basics in a school set up on the base. There, the curriculum he helped devise included the theory, operation and maintenance of electrical and radio equipment. The GIs even learned to rebuild

Japanese radio receiving and transmitting devices as part of this program.

In the official military discharge paperwork filled out in Camp Chaffee, Ark., the Army had listed four steps of training, all of which would help Dick in his career in some way: Signal Corps basic training, radio operator, radio instructor, and perhaps most of all, radio repairman training. The specialized work involved installing and operating tactical field radios (both transmitting and receiving), sending and receiving messages by Morse Code, semaphore, light signals, tone signals and voice, installing, inspecting, testing and repairing amplitude-modulated radio transmitting and receiving equipment, using testing equipment such as voltmeters, ohmmeters, tube testers and oscilloscopes. With these, such specialists often used a drill press, soldering iron and other tools. Many of these skills would come into play hundreds of times in Dick's future work. Providence was operative.

Not only that, but his advanced training in Missouri and Georgia provided him specialized study in signal communication, message center procedure and cryptology, radio signaling and wire communication. He also had "practical training in organization and use of communication equipment used within a division signal system," according to his Army paperwork. Over the course of his military career, Dick also would learn installation, maintenance and operation of air-ground communication systems, radio field nets, phone and telegraph systems. He even studied the types of wire used and practiced making common wire splices. Again, these were skill sets he would use countless times in future years as he would start up and grow his business.

Yet, Dick often had something, or rather someone, else on his mind, in addition to electronics during his war years, namely Jinnie. When he left the Army, he and Jinnie were married in 1946 and moved to Atlanta so Dick could continue his education at Georgia Tech.

Their first apartment had beaver-board walls, concrete floors and a pot-bellied stove, but they were on their way up because their next apartment had concrete walls and portable closets. Decades later in the 1970s, Jinnie would recall in a company newsletter that they had lived on just $91 a month, about $1,500 in today's dollars. To supplement their income, Dick took photographs and Jinnie baked birthday cakes. She later got a job with an electronics distributor in Atlanta.

During these early newlywed years, though, the couple still found time to have fun with the many mutual hobbies and interests they shared. The two worked together to build their first TV set when these were just coming onto the market. Their first one worked and they then built one for Dick's father. "We had pictures in the Atlanta Journal Constitution of our soldering the sets," Dick said. When Atlanta's WSB station came on the air, Dick and Jinnie were ready for the first TV show in the city.

Both also were interested in ham radio operations to the extent that Jinnie learned Morse Code and earned her ham license, too.

When Dick was graduated from Georgia Tech in 1950, not many companies were recruiting engineers and the opportunities were not robust, to say the least. "Usually, a lot of companies would come visit the college to recruit, but that year, only about one did," he said.

Because Dick needed a job, he and Jinnie came home to Dick's family's lumber business in Belzoni, Mississippi, with the words, "Dad, I'm your son, you've got to hire me." Dick enjoyed his work at the sawmill. "I was working outside and doing mechanical work, welding some gear and generally keeping stuff put together and repaired," Dick said. "I was happy. It felt like I was earning my keep when I was working there. The hunting and fishing were great in that area of the Delta, too. We were early in our marriage and had our son, Rick, who was born in 1952."

Once in the Delta, the couple learned to fly and soloed the same day. Soon after, they bought a little Cessna. Jinnie recalled the fun the couple had with the plane in a letter she wrote to an old college friend in 1995. "It was almost a necessity (to) partake of the unique social life in the Delta," she wrote. "A friend would call and invite us over. They might live 40 miles away. We would hop into the plane, fly over and land in their pasture. Or we would fly over and land on a sandbar on the Mississippi River to meet a group of friends and cook breakfast. I would fly up to Memphis to go shopping or to Jackson, Mississippi to the hairdresser."

Dick spent nine years at the family sawmill. While he was there, as a hobby he built a ham radio tower 60 feet tall with pipes that formed a triangle-shaped structure for support. These pieces he welded together with cross braces. A hinge was built at the bottom for pulling the tower up vertically.

He worked up and down the sawmill line not as a supervisor but as a general labor employee who also did some lumber grading. The major part of Dick's job was to scale the logs when they came in the log trucks and determine how much footage of hardwood was arriving. The lumber they made was sold to furniture and flooring manufacturers. It was a standard building practice in that era that hardwood floors were installed in most of the homes, so that helped buoy the business.

Dick was finished with work by 3 p.m. most days and often went fishing with a friend from the mill. They also enjoyed rigging up jeeps and bought three of them along the way. Each of the two had a jeep of his own and they used a third one for spare parts for the better one. They'd attach winches and boat rigs on the jeeps so they could also use them when they went fishing.

The somewhat idyllic life in the Mississippi Delta ended when Dick's father died in 1956, an event that precipitated their move to Memphis. After his father's death, Dick needed to take care of the family business from the main sales office.

"In Memphis as I took over the family business, we had a two-person sales office in the Commerce Title Building on Main Street," he recalled. The office had been established by Dick's grandfather and was called the C.P. Bodine Lumber Co. The office staff also oversaw the company's hardwood sawmill in Belzoni, where Dick had earlier worked.

The family business had a history that reached back to Dick's grandfather, Cooper P. Bodine, for whom the business was named. Cooper P. Bodine, who was born in Paris, Mo., and received his early education there, was active in organizing the Memphis Sash & Door Co. in 1904, the year the Bodine family moved to Memphis. In 1929, the grandfather and company founder died of a sudden heart attack while at work in his office.

The history of the family business, which was handed down through three generations, is inextricably intertwined with the history of Dick's family members and their lives. Dick's mother, Mary Budd Stewart Bodine, was born in Memphis, while his father, Richard Sr., was from Shelbina, Missouri. Mary Bodine's father, David Wood Stewart, journeyed to this country from Ireland at age 18 and went to work for the firm of Gwynne & Co. in New Orleans. Three years later, he became a member of the same firm in Memphis. David Stewart later married Bessie Norton of Memphis and they lived in one of the stately old homes on Court Avenue near a former residence of Confederate President Jefferson Davis. They had three children: Mary Budd, Elizabeth, and Norton Stewart.

Dick's own father had moved to Memphis with his family as a 9-year-old. He attended the University of Virginia, but he left the university to become a Navy aviator during World War I. A 1940 president of the Lumberman's Club, Mr. Bodine Sr. also had worked in the cotton business and served as president of Memphis Cotton Carnival Association the same year. When there wasn't enough activity in the lumber business to keep Mr.

Bodine Sr.'s interest over time, he turned to the cotton business. Dick's father would return to the sawmill business after his father, its founder, died.

Among his family members, his grandmother, Annie E. Bodine, was something of a pioneer as a woman managing a business in Memphis in the early 20th century. In addition to managing the lumber company until she died in 1937, she also had worked as a secretary-treasurer of the Southern Compress and Warehouse Co.

After Dick's own father died, he stayed at the Commerce Title business in Downtown Memphis for three or four years.

"All business was made on the phone; your word was your bond," he said. "If someone agreed to sell at a certain price in the future, you would never back off of that."

Still, the work was not really enough to keep him busy. He often could sell an entire month's production supply very quickly. Technically, a salesman could sell more, but the sawmill at a given time would produce only so much.

Dick was dealing with people he knew who were, for the most part, reliable individuals. The lumber business was like a little fraternity, he recalled, although he sold around the country and shipped the cut wood by railroad over long distances.

"As far as real fulfillment, the work at an office in Memphis was completely different," he said. "I would get to work midmorning, pour some coffee, come back and make a sale, read a magazine and then go play golf. It would sound like an ideal situation unless you get in it and just get bored." To mix it up and review new products and volume, he went down to the sawmill every other week for three days at a time.

"Again, I was just bored, didn't like what I was doing at the sales office," Dick said. "I didn't know much about the lumber business. It wasn't my cup of tea. We had a chance to rent the sawmill out. We did that for a year and then sold it to a friendly competitor."

The sawmill, too, wound down operations over a period of some seven years; part was sold and part closed down. The new property owners made a catfish pond out of it and it later became part of Belzoni's growing status of becoming a catfish capital. With the proceeds from the sale of the family lumber business, the money went to Dick's mother who died in her mid-80s.

In 1961, Dick and Jinnie found themselves at a crossroads – one of many they would encounter. Again, it was time to decide just what to do next.

Building the Company
—from Chicken Coop to Collierville

A FTER PROVING HIMSELF THROUGH HIS initial years inthe family lumber business, Dick increasingly found that thework was losing the challenge and appeal it once had held. That acted as a kind of catalyst for him to venture into new avenues for a livelihood. He would start his own enterprise, he vowed.

"I had been tinkering with electronics all my life. Jinnie and I were both ham radio operators as hobbyists at home," he said. "Ever since we came to Memphis, we were looking for something to do (beyond the family lumber business). We had a friend in North Carolina who was constructing a new house there. We told him that we could install the intercom system he had bought for his new home. While driving up there, we talked more and more about a new direction we could take to making a living. By the end of the trip, we both agreed on the idea of making good intercoms and selling them as a true possibility."

The couple returned to Memphis after that successful initial venture. They then decided to start investigating other companies' intercom systems. These generally were intercoms with music combinations. They weren't great intercoms; about all one could say is that users could talk and hear through them.

"Jinnie and I thought of ways we could build better ones and really have something to sell," Dick said. "When we got back to Memphis, we started talking about it further and calling on people we knew who were building new houses."

Soon afterward, the renowned inner ear specialist, Dr. John Shea, heard someone talking about the fact that the Bodines were venturing into this new field. The Shea home on Shady Grove Road became the first local house they wired for a custom intercom system.

Dick and Jinnie had been living on their mutual savings, which had started to dwindle with trickling business, but that early order helped plant the seeds for the Bodine Co., which started in 1962 out of the garage and chicken coop at the couple's Germantown home they'd purchased three years earlier. The Bodines had bought 10 acres on Dogwood Road, partly as a place to keep his sister's horse. On this acreage were a nice house, barn, chicken coop and smoke house. The young company would operate out of these quarters for its first five years. Over time, they remodeled the chicken coop for production and used the barn for storage. "The chicken coop" became a favorite oft-quoted bit of Bodine company lore.

Business was slow at the start and the savings were thin, but the desire to succeed was too strong for them to ignore. "We figured if we could sell one full intercom system a month, we could survive," Dick recalled.

The couple soon started calling on more of their friends and architects who were building larger homes and who saw both the usefulness and novelty of being able to communicate readily with family members across sprawling residences.

"We had a suitcase that we put a piece of prefinished plywood on one side and mounted the intercoms which showcased what we provided," Dick said. "We had another display board with a remote unit that we could place in another room and demonstrate the intercoms. Most had seen the combination of music-with-intercom, but when we demonstrated the quality and look of the custom intercoms, people could see their (enhanced) value and that helped make for a fairly easy sale," Dick said.

The wall-mounted intercoms were on Plexiglas® faceplates. In each room, the Bodines would select the same paint to match the rooms and apply that to the units. They made other units out of walnut, if they were to rest on a desk or bookshelf.

From the start, the Bodines used their own units rather than those from other manufactures. "Most people had never heard a really good intercom," Dick said. "A majority of the (existing) intercoms had that little humming sound, but these were dead quiet (in the idle mode). Ours also were a fair amount more expensive. The look and audio quality were the winning tickets. Labeling on the units permitted anyone to talk directly to any other room and they had customized directories on the faceplates. We didn't integrate radios with these intercoms, but we did come up with independent music systems." The music system also was unique in that the homeowner could turn it on, but no music came out anywhere, unless the control panel was activated.

The lion's share, then, of Bodine Co.'s earliest business was derived from that type of work. At that time, the company charged $1,300 for an entire system. "We always had good margins, but I was not getting paid for the time I put into development," Dick said. "At first, I sold them, built them and installed them. We didn't really bargain, either, on installations. If you didn't want it, you didn't want it."

The reputation of the devices and systems grew as time went on. The Bodines even derived some intercom business from as far away as Little Rock.

At this juncture, the young startup business would get its second right-hand man. "I was roughing in the wiring on a hot July day in 1963," Dick recalled. "Jinnie had driven back to our house in Germantown. An applicant named Jim Cagle was driving up the driveway and said he was looking for a job. She said, 'wait here' and she drove back into Memphis where I was. We discussed his needing a job and decided that maybe it was time to hire somebody. Either we were going to have to miss some possible sales or put on some more help.

Jinnie went back out and brought him to where I was climbing around rafters, drilling holes and running wires in a house. I was hot and sweaty. I said, 'This is what it is, you are in and out of attics, basements and everywhere else. This is what you'll be getting into. Are you sure you want it?' " He said 'yes' to starting at $2 an hour. Shortly thereafter, Jim moved his wife and baby from California and became the first employee of the Bodine Co."

Those early years are filled with memories such as Jim's aversion to crawling under homes for fear of snakes and one snake that crawled up onto the resin bucket and got stuck. On another day, they found a nest full of baby mice in a drawer of their parts cabinet.

Jim later would become production manager, and after 33 years in various positions, he retired from Bodine in 2008. He still remembers details from the day he was hired. "I looked in the phone book for anybody in electronics and went up to the house. I just drove in the driveway. I met Jinnie and she took me back to the house and asked me to wait. She went and got Dick and he was on a job. She took me to where he was working and that was the interview."

At the time, Dick was working on the home of Billy Dunavant, who would one day come to own the largest private cotton merchandising enterprise in the world, also with headquarters in Memphis. "We worked very hard and busily, but it was like a family," recalled the company's first secretary, Mary Nell McCool, who was hired a few years later. She found out about the job in about 1966 when the Bodine family would come into her

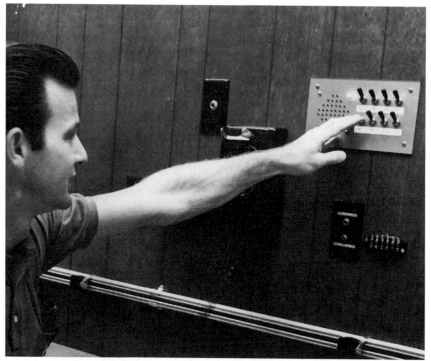

Jim Cagle with one of the intercoms. The intercoms were the staple product of the early business.

former father-in-law's grocery store, McCool's at Poplar Avenue and Highland Street. Her relative told her that Jinnie was looking for an assistant, so Mary Nell went by and talked with Dick and Jinnie and left there with a job.

"All of us worked as a unit," Mary Nell said. "Jinnie and I were in the office's glassed-in sun porch at the house. We kept equipment in a room of the house and also in the barn and the chicken coop."

Their desks faced an expansive back yard. One other piece of furniture had an unusual history. It was a table that started off as a piano Jinnie had inherited. She wanted the rear leg cut off one day and after some handiwork with employee Jim Cagle's saw, it was fashioned into a hall table.

"My most vivid memory was feeling like Jinnie and Dick were my family," Mary Nell said. "That overrode all other memories and was the most important thing to me. Their son, Rick, was a great kid. He would help Dick and Jim in assembling things. He was talented."

One longtime friend, Claude McCord, an MIT engineering grad who married Dick's first cousin, said many years later, "I never dreamed that all those resistors, capacitators, transistors, coils of wire and soldering irons that adorned the furniture in your sunroom would ever amount to anything more than a hobby."

Rick would help out during school breaks. He put in full work days and was really proud of what he accomplished during the day. He often would find Jinnie to take her back and show her what he'd done.

Dick's mother would come by and everyone would have lunch in the dining room of the house. "Even during lunch, we'd sit around, talk about the business, trouble shoot or throw ideas out of what we were trying to accomplish," Mary Nell said. "Dick would brainstorm about something and scratch his head and someone would throw some ideas out and everyone would then look at each other and say, 'That might work!'"

So the little group was a creative problem-solving team in motion. If something new came up, they would talk about it and sit there brainstorming until all of a sudden, there would be that "Aha" moment.

The early staff members did whatever they had to do to make the little company go. Dick would go out and get the business, come back and then figure out how to make it work. Jinnie was an asset all around. She ran the business while Dick would do the inventing, for the most part. The fact that Jinnie was the CEO handling most business decisions and Dick was serving as

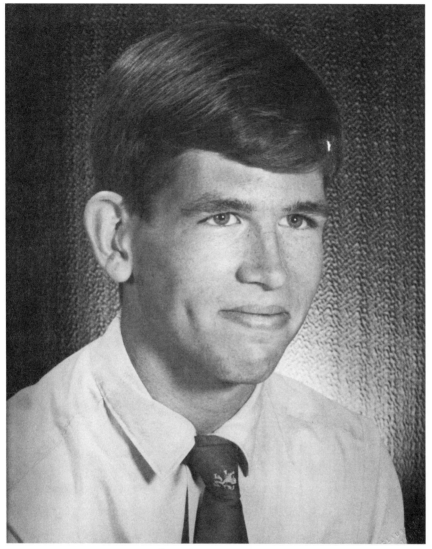

Rick Bodine as a teenager.

product development manager provided a balance so they could discuss mutual concerns and work them out.

Although business was not robust by any means in the early years, there weren't many slow weeks as a whole. "We were always working up products, even when we didn't have active orders,"

Dick said. "We were always fairly busy." He'd call on customers often at nighttime and would build day and night.

Jim Cagle, though, does recall a few slow moments here and there. "On boring days, we'd shoot squirrels out of the pecan tree," he said. But the squirrels weren't harassed that often. Dick and his fledgling staff were too engaged in building up the early company's foundation.

In time, the difference in Dick's enjoyment of life became evident to himself and Jinnie. "I finally got into something I really loved," he said years later with an enthusiasm that showed in his voice.

Another one of Bodine Co.'s key early specialty jobs was completed for a restaurant that rotated in the top round floor of White Station Tower, the first East Memphis high-rise. Built in the mid 1960s, White Station Tower was a bold move for entrepreneur Buck Clark. When it was first conceived, architectural plans didn't have the well-known circular top in their renderings, according to a February 2008 Memphis magazine article. However, by the time construction began, revolving restaurants were all the rage. The 22-story structure offered 343,000 square feet of floor space top to bottom.

The Embers restaurant there took a leisurely two hours and five minutes to make a complete rotation. All the same, the restaurant managers needed a board with lights to show which tables had been served and their locations. Any waiter could be confused by coming out of the kitchen and having his table revolve from the 12 o'clock position, for instance, to the 4 o'clock position. Bodine's solution was to place four readouts spaced 90 degrees apart around the inner wall of the restaurant. "We built these readouts so that when you served a table, you pushed a button to let all of the waiters also know that a given table had been served," Dick said. "When they left, you could push another button to let the busboys know. There was a lot of wiring involved."

Jim Cagle played an instrumental role in the wiring work. "I sat down for hours wiring those cables into it," Jim attested.

The restaurant later became known for a time as The Pyrenees. Today, the dome houses executive offices that no longer revolve.

That early venture was yet another example of a one-time, one-use product that was not duplicated. It was to be the first of many, following that singular-use business model. That kind of customer service became known as a hallmark strategy for the company and one which added to its reputation.

The next big turn came when the Bodines secured the RCA account, which was setting up a factory in Memphis during the early 1960s to build color television sets. Bodine was still building intercoms then, even as it started to design and build custom testing equipment for RCA to quality check the TVs it made.

As an electrical engineer, Dick designed, built, sold and installed not only the intercoms, but also some of the other equipment the company was turning out, such as custom burglar alarm systems. Meanwhile, Jinnie's oversight of the business office also called for her to master the accounting and administrative end.

"She was a very strong woman," Dick said. "My ability covered how to conceptualize products and how to build them, making them work. I was into improving and innovating all the time. Jinnie knew how to run administrative operations, both when the company was small and when it grew much larger in size." Their synergies and skill sets worked like good math.

All of his life, Dick had liked to fix things and still does. He is still a hands-on man. His mother always said that his father could hardly change a light bulb, but Dick grew up enjoying the idea of constructing and rebuilding things.

Around the time the Bodines won the contract to build test equipment for the then-new RCA plant in Memphis, they realized they needed more space. They started by remodeling the chicken coop in their Germantown backyard into a working area and used their barn for storage.

There were still other promising products that would soon far surpass the promise of the early ones, though, and like many innovations, the company's cornerstone invention would emerge through a request by a customer.

Around 1965, Dick heard through the grapevine that local advertising executive Tom O'Ryan was looking for a way to illuminate signs on buses so that they could be seen at night and draw attention to Southland Greyhound Park, one of Tom's clients. The challenge, then, was to design a circuit that would operate fluorescent lights from low-voltage DC. The idea for the Bodines' most successful product thus was born - a battery-powered fluorescent fixture, which they called the *Tran*-BAL® - short for transistorized ballast. Today, many taxis and buses have lighted advertising signs and one can walk into certain electronics stores now and buy the components and find a schematic to build this type product. However, back then, it was a state-of-the-art, leading-edge technology. The resulting *Tran*-BAL® made that unusual request possible and about 100 of these devices were sold to the advertising executive.

This *Tran*-BAL® device had started out as a small sea foam-green unit. Not many advertising lighting units were actually sold, although that very idea helped launch the product that Dick devised from scratch.

"In order to make use of the ability to operate a fluorescent lamp from low-voltage DC current, we packaged a *Tran*-BAL® with a charger and 12-volt battery," Dick explained. "This afterward became the first attempt to make the fixture work as an emergency light. This was way too big and heavy to be practical, but it started us on the path to developing what would turn out later to become the company's (longstanding and) major product line." That development – inverter ballasts that operate fluorescent lamps from DC power instead of AC current — thus would form its core technology. In developing these, the company was able to arrive at the proper inner circuitry for the highly specialized fluorescent lamps to come off its assembly lines.

Initially, however, the fledgling company almost made what would have been the biggest mistake of its life. "Because of its initial lack of popularity, we almost dropped pursuing it in the beginning," Dick said. "Then, one time, we got orders for one of these seven days in a row. Selling one $20 item a day for seven days may not be the way to get rich, but it did renew our faith in it."

The resulting innovative ballast would trigger most other products the company has developed since. Since the early ballasts it used were too big and bulky, Dick worked on making them small enough to go into various fixtures. Manufacturers must have UL approval for products that go into commercial buildings, which means the equipment has undergone extensive tests.

"We went to Underwriters Laboratories, and they had no procedure for evaluating these products of ours because no one was making them in quantity. GE, meanwhile, had gone to UL with similar specs and asked for UL-approval," Dick said. "They were big enough to warrant that. UL then took that and developed specs for it. Then, we could make ours to meet the newly authorized specs.

"GE led us to believe orders would be pouring in. That didn't happen. GE said if we could make one of these economically feasible, then they would not get in the business. They reneged and got in the business anyway, but all of that process actually helped us meet the UL listings. GE later got out of the business."

Meanwhile, the wheels in Dick's inventive mind were still turning. "Deep down, we thought there could be a growing market for a fixture to keep a lamp on during a power failure," Dick said. He was quite right, although the company's heyday would yet arrive on the calendar for a waiting marketplace. That in itself was an ahead-of-the-curve notion. Bodine Co., though, constantly innovated to meet a future market demand.

"We didn't try to patent a lot," Dick said. "It would have been difficult to defend patents and we were changing things so rapidly. If someone tried to copy something we were doing, we would beat them because we were two steps ahead of them."

Although the *Tran*-BAL® did not move rapidly off the shelves at first, Dick wanted and needed to stay busy, so he dually focused on RCA for a number of years. If it were not for that RCA business in the early years of the Bodine Co., it might have ended right there.

How did such a youthful startup come to serve that large-scale business? Bodine Co. often had bought electronic parts from Bluff City Distributing Co., doing business as Bluff City Electronics, and RCA did too. One day, Glenn Cowles, then a manager at Bluff City Distributing, mentioned to one of the RCA engineers that the Bodine Co. might be a good outfit to build their testing equipment. The account would soon become the Bodine Company's first truly big customer.

Once the early agreement was reached, Dick would order parts from Bluff City, then Glenn's brother, Alfred Cowles would bring the parts home and one of the Bodines would pick up the parts at his front porch, the Cowles family recalled. Glenn came to be vice president of purchasing at Bluff City and Alfred was president. Glenn also was the primary contact at Bluff City with RCA.

If an entity is going to run a production line of television sets, there are certain testing devices it must have. That meant the engineer in charge of building this RCA plant would go to the Bodine Co. with drawings and schematics of what was needed and Bodine would provide quotes on building those.

We called this the final inspection before delivery of some of the equipment made for the then-new RCA television plant in Memphis. This is Dick Bodine with Blaze, the horse outside the chicken coop on the Germantown back-property. The building in the background is the horse's stable.

"Every wire internally would be the same on all these units in order to facilitate maintenance," Dick said. "In providing their required testing equipment, we had to build transmitters for each TV channel to send signals out to the production floor."

Deliveries to the RCA plant at first were made via the Bodine's station wagon. If the order had to be shipped out of town, it was mailed.

Jinnie had some vivid memories of the early times as described in her 1995 letter: "We had a lot of fun in those days. We thoroughly enjoyed an irreverent attitude toward the hotshot, big-company engineers. Building their very expensive precision equipment in a converted chicken coop was hard enough for them to take, but then we sent them pictures of the final inspection – our two horses looking in the rear doors at the equipment as it was being loaded into the station wagon for delivery!"

It was that very combination of down-home sophistication mixed with good-natured humor that would mark the Bodines' business relationship for years.

For design and quality control purposes, Dick traveled early in the process to the RCA plant in Indianapolis to study the units. "We got into the room and the engineer would let me look at their units but not touch them. The screen room was where all the transmitters were mounted and there were color bar generators. There was rack after rack. The big room was electromagnetically shielded from the outside because it was important that unwanted signals not get in or out of the room."

The RCA scenario would prove in yet other ways to be an instrumental milestone in the survival of the company. These involved bank loans, paying salaries and an 11th-hour Godsend.

Around this time, the Bodine Co. attained the RCA business, Jinnie talked with an unnamed bank officer to ask for a $25,000 line of credit. The bank loan officer called her and said he'd taken it to the board and gained approval. Shortly after that, the company started building RCA equipment. Jinnie would pay workers at the end of each week in the early days. That practice went on for a number of weeks.

"We had a payroll coming up the next Tuesday and she called the bank and said, 'I need some more money.' The banker replied, 'You have borrowed $13,000, and unless you put up some more collateral, that is all you can get.' He had never gone to the board with it as he had told us."

That spelled panic time for a young business. The Bodines knew that would mean a real crimp in the company if they couldn't meet the payroll. Monday morning, the first check from RCA, one for $6,000, arrived and more money then started coming in. Right away, Jinnie began dealing with a new bank. When the company amassed about $13,000, it was able to pay off the initial bank and stopped borrowing money from that time forward.

Only one day from disaster, the Bodines had received their first real account receivable. "After we met payroll and paid off the bank, we just decided it was better to earn interest on our money than pay on it," Dick said. "Everything after that was generated out of house funds because we came so close to getting sunk the first time."

Although the Bodine Co. still was operating out of a house and adjoining property that was not to be for much longer. One morning, the not-yet-fully-dressed couple had to open their door to an equipment salesman. After he left, Jinnie said, "That is it! We are going to have to build a plant." They had four full-time employees at the time — Jim Cagle, Dick, Jinnie and Mary Nell McCool. The Bodines bought three acres in Collierville in 1967 for $6,000 and soon started to build the first building with about 4,000 square feet, about the size of a spacious residence.

The Bodines found Collierville to be amenable enough to new businesses at the time. Early work was derived from orders for intercoms, music systems and any specialized devices requested by customers. "We just had an almost empty building at first," Dick said. "We knew we had to swim hard because you might drown. Just three offices, including a spare one, some work tables and a lab were there at first."

"Collierville was interested in having us; there was very little else out there. I had mixed emotions about it because I loved going to the house. At the same time, we were expanding so we needed to go to a much larger facility to handle what we were doing at that point."

One part of the early business that did provide spotty income, nevertheless did not flourish for very long: the burglar and security alarm business. A 1960s article in The Commercial Appeal told of its economically priced K-13 Intruder Alarm system, which gave it a status of being the only manufacturer of burglar alarms in this area. Home Telephone Co. of Olive Branch had thought there could be a demand for a burglar alarm system linked with the use of telephone lines, so Dick did his research and fabricated a product that could be linked by leased phone line auditory circuits. It then sold this to independent phone companies via Bodine distributors in Tennessee, Mississippi and Kentucky.

However, in that day, such a system still was a bit ahead of its time and just didn't enjoy the market demand it does now. At that time, the burglar alarm part of the business didn't even pay for itself. To try to give it more exposure, though, the company went out on a bit of a limb and had a TV commercial filmed to promote its alarm systems. A person who was dressed up in a striped top to look like a prisoner was supposed to be filmed sneaking in through the ceiling to drop onto the safe in Jinnie's old office. Unfortunately, the first "take" didn't go quite as planned as the burglar lost balance and fell through the ceiling into an empty office. Of course, the scene had to be reshot.

This line was subsequently disbanded after Dick put up with enough after-hours calls about systems going off, either by accident or because of break-ins. He ended up selling that segment to Frase-Uhlhorn, based in Memphis.

Some time later, and after the Bodine operation was transplanted and rooted in Collierville, business with RCA returned. Rather than building equipment to use in its Memphis plant, Bodine Co. began refurbishing products for RCA's facility in Taiwan.

RCA would send its parts to Memphis so Bodine Co. could recondition them like new. In the corporate process, RCA closed about five plants in the states and had loads of used equipment it wanted to use in its Taiwanese plant. The only problem was that only new equipment was allowed there. "RCA was faced with a

*Rick, Jinnie, salesman, Jim Cagle and Dick at an early industry expo,
a crucial showcase in the early growth phases of a young Bodine Co.*

dilemma of making that equipment new," Dick said. "We would take it and convert it into pristine condition. It amounted to a lot of commercially built testing equipment."

Jim Cagle, meanwhile, had his own vivid memories of the chapter in the company chronicles. "When RCA decided to move operations out of the country, we found out a year and a half in advance," Jim said. "RCA started delivering equipment to us to be refurbished and sent it to Taiwan and we gained a lot of business through that."

Jinnie was also Bodine Co.'s chief inspector at that time, going over completed units with a fine-toothed comb, especially the RCA equipment. She could spot something wrong immediately. She went over each item or process in the plant that was critical to anything going out the door. For the RCA product destined for

The relay rack that was put together by a couple of RCA engineers to be shipped to Taiwan. They requested a key to the plant so they could show their bosses what they had done. After they left for the day, we added a few things of our own. This is what they saw when they walked in.

Taiwan, she also had to become an expert on Taiwanese customs requirements. As it would happen, Jinnie's brother Jack, many years later, would be a manager of RCA's Government and Commercial Systems in New Jersey, according to a Bodine newsletter.

Still, the Collierville iteration of the company continued to strive financially for the period, although the RCA refurbishing business was not as lucrative as the earlier RCA test equipment scenario.

Jim, who was instrumental on that project and many others for years to come as Dick's right-hand man, was a key player in the growing business. Whatever Dick was building or installing, Jim would be working on the same thing.

Navy service technician trainers from Millington were brought in to help with the specialty assembly work. As electronics instructors, the "chiefs" became indispensable. In the early days, especially, the projects would not have happened without them. That didn't in itself make every day an easy day — even with the "chiefs" to help out. Once, there was a snowstorm for four days and the couple had no power at their home in Germantown, so they got sleeping bags and slept in the plant. Because of the snowstorm, the Millington technicians at first didn't want to come in. They called and said the weather was too bad. "Our office staff all managed to get there," Mary Nell said. "We told them, 'We need you.' It was crunch time trying to get that equipment out. I said, 'I will come pick you all up.' They said, 'no, no,' and they decided they could get there on their own after all." While the number varied, the company used four regular technicians from Millington and two or three extras.

Meanwhile, the young company also was pursuing a variety of collateral business that came in the door. One day, a crop duster pilot walked in and wanted the team to devise a gauge that could tell him how much chemical content he still had left in his tanks at any given point. Dick designed one for him.

"About 15 years later, the pilot wanted another one and called me, but I told him that was so long ago, I was sorry I just couldn't remember how to build another one," Dick said, laughing. "When a customer had a problem, we figured out how to solve it, but that was one of the few times we couldn't help someone again."

There was other agricultural specialty work in the mix, as well. For the U.S. Department of Agriculture, the Bodine Co. created a device that was placed in special crop pest traps out in the field. They controlled an ultraviolet light that would attract the insects. "We had a device to take the battery voltage and raise it to electrocuting voltage (for insects). They would put these in the field and go sample the insects."

As Jim Cagle described it, the device would be placed in the field with the *Tran*-BAL® connected to a battery and the device would attract bugs at night. "They would die, fall into the funnel and the research workers would count the desired ones versus the bad ones," he said. They were developing sprays that they wanted to kill specific insects, but not all insects."

Through the early life of the company, there were some light moments. Once, a couple of visiting engineers were mounting equipment on 6-foot high relay racks. They worked at the plant all day and wanted to show their bosses their progress. A Bodine employee gave them the key to the plant and after they left, Jim Cagle called Dick and said, "What do you see?" Dick looked and saw that the Bodine employees had dressed the relay rack up to look like a comical robot to throw the visiting engineers and their bosses for a loop. The oscilloscopes looked like eyeballs. When it was shipped to Taiwan, it was boxed up to look like a coffin. The "robot" even got an artificial rose for the voyage.

All the while, the company kept building intercoms for a number of years until it got too busy with other work. In addition, the key replacement builder for the intercoms, a former B-52 pilot, finally quit. This was the final terminus for the Bodine Co. turning out intercoms after a good long run. Remarkably, an original Bodine intercom customer 40 years later in 2009 found Dick in Memphis through some phone call connections, urgently saying he needed help fixing his unit. Dick tossed some tools into a Zip lock bag, went over to the East Memphis house off of Yates and half an hour later, the problem was fixed!

As Bodine Co. began to grow, time confirmed that Dick and Jinnie were wise in dividing responsibilities of authority and not to second guess each other. Each needed a territory to supervise. Jinnie oversaw operations and Dick headed product development. Part of this plan called for a sales team. The couple hired a quick succession of sales managers, then hired David Crippen, a man who, over the ensuing years, would become one of the mainstays of the company's success.

By the time David Crippen arrived, the Bodine Co. was already in the emergency lighting business and he changed the way the company handled problems. Over time, he unmistakably influenced how the company maintained its customer base.

"Not only would we take care of their problems, we'd do anything to solve those situations for them," David said.

"Jinnie decided we needed somebody who knew about marketing and we selected David," Dick said. Dick and Jinnie's talents were chiefly in the fields of invention and business management — but not sales. That is precisely where David came into the game plan.

Not long after the sales director arrived, the phone rang with a job problem and David went to Jinnie. He told her what happened and asked what to do about it. Jinnie replied, 'That is your problem. That is why we hired you – do not ask me.' David solved that and all other similar problems eventually.

Soon afterward, he instituted a procedure stating that regardless of who called or what the problem was, Bodine Co. would do everything necessary to fix it. "We told him at first, 'You could break us doing that'," Dick said. David replied, "No, this is what we need to do." It is what we have done ever since. In fact, it became a major policy of the company to take care of the customer's problem.

Dick likens the scenario to an electrician who is on a job and who has products that might not work and he's upset because he wants to finish the job. The first question David's sales department would ask is what could be done to fix it, regardless of what it was. And if it was a technical problem, they would have an engineer consult with the customer.

"David was very instrumental in moving the company forward," Jim attested. "He had an MBA and that helped. He had a good ability in social situations too. David often got customer input and called on our reps in the field for additional ideas to build the business."

Sales were administered in-house at this time and the sales manager started to build the representative network. David was the first one to accomplish any sustained marketing efforts at the company. Even so, it faced two problems. Bodine was a small outfit, with a limited product, which made it difficult to get a really good sales representative interested at the beginning. There were not yet enough products for potential sales reps to reap substantial commissions. "We'd go to Chicago to a convention and meet with a rep network," Dick said. "They had not heard of Bodine. You had to sell it to them first before they would sell it to the world."

However, marketing per se was not a major concentrated effort in the early days by any means. The company didn't do formal advertising, for the most part, but Jinnie would place a few small ads in business publications. The *Tran*-BAL® received articles in trade journals, which helped get the word out.

"I never liked to travel, so I didn't want to go to a lot of trade shows," Dick said. The company did construct a homemade booth, though, that some of its salesmen carried to such shows.

Beth Hoople, who later spent 10 years in the marketing department with David Crippen as a manager, remembers what excellent people skills the Bodines found when they hired him. My first week or so there, David mentioned that he'd always found it easier to tell the truth than to lie, because you had to remember what you said when you lied; if you told the truth, all you needed to do was remember the truth," she said. "For some reason, I'd never heard that truism before, and at the beginning of my professional life, it sounded like such great advice for dealing with the business world."

One of David's favorite expressions was, "When you point the finger of blame at someone else." (Here he'd point his index finger) "You have to notice that there are three fingers pointing back at yourself."

For the few missteps, miscalculations or bad decisions that the marketing team might make, it reminded all to analyze the who, what, where, when and why of a situation — simply to assess how to avoid repeating the mistake, Beth said. "Attempting to analyze who was to blame, or on whom to assign blame, wasted valuable time and resources."

"Mostly, I remember the time I was interviewed for the job," Beth said. "David spent a few minutes making sure I was comfortable and then apologized profusely because interviewing candidates was not his strong suit, and he wasn't sure he'd do it well. Then, we spent the better part of an hour discussing specifications and expectations of the position in a logical, organized manner that proved he indeed was an excellent interviewer."

David also began a program as the company grew of having "Breakfast with the Boss." As discussions about job benefits, work hours, procedures, and rules sometimes led to thinly-veiled complaints that working eight hours a day, five days a week was sometimes no picnic, he'd nod agreeably. "You're right," he'd say with a smile. "When we get right down to it, no matter what we might do to make it fun — ping-pong tables, parties, whatever, Work Is Work." From the way David Crippen said it, you could hear the capital letters on those words: Work Is Work.

It was evident that there was not a time when David didn't express respect and admiration for Dick and Jinnie, the way they ran the business, and his gratitude for their respect and admiration for him.

Meanwhile, Bodine kept improving the product line and then it all grew together. "As it grew, it makes it all the easier to promote. As you get to be top dog, you acquire good reps clamoring to represent you," Dick said. "Once we had the nationwide reps set up, if it went in their area, they got credit and commissions off of it. At this point, we were taking orders for anything. We would take minimum orders of one."

While a unique product idea contributed to the success of the Bodine Co., Dick and Jinnie's benevolently paternalistic management style was equally important. Bodine employees were treated as an extended family. Dick often said, "All other competitors have buildings, equipment and technology similar to ours, but they don't have our employees. They are the unique ingredient that makes us better than the rest." That is also part of the reason there is such little turnover with employees who tend to work at the business for at least 10 or 15 years.

Several new insights were gained as time went on in terms of how the married couple operated the helm of the business ship and at the same time maintained a clear delineation of authority between their respective jobs.

"She knew that side of the business and I knew what I do not understand," Dick said. "It left me free for what I really love – research and development."

Jinnie had her own take on it, as she stated in her 1995 letter: "I had much to learn, especially about accounting and finance. I remember getting out my old textbooks and notes from Northwestern University. The first few years, I kept the books and would turn them over to a CPA at the end of the year to prepare the tax returns and the annual report. He would come back, throw the books on my desk and growl, 'You made money! Where is it?!' I nearly died of fright every time. For self-preservation, I took accounting courses at night school and later, to learn more about managing a company, attended many seminars given by the American Management Association, mostly in New York."

Jinnie was an extremely disciplined woman. During conversations with employees at lunch hour, she on occasion had a cigarette in her hand. The anti-smoking movement had begun in earnest among health-care advocates and the tide was beginning to turn against smoking being trendy or cool. Jinnie looked ruefully at the cigarette in her hand, sounding extremely chagrined as she would explain, "This is my 'candy bar' for the day." One never doubted that if she were limiting herself to one, two, or three a day, that was all she smoked. There would be no cheating.

All was not seriousness and the company had a real sense of humor all along, Jim said. "That set it apart and made it easier to work there. We kidded Dick and he learned to laugh at his own mistakes after a while, too."

The company in the late 1960s was beginning to get a few orders for the emergency lights. With David on board, sales slowly started building up. His favorite phrase for the marketing team was NHUS3: Nothing Happens Until Someone Sells Something.

It was a busy time. Dick and Jinnie worked as many or more hours than anybody else. They would work until dinnertime and get something to eat on the way home. Often, they would just go to bed when they got home, get up the next morning and go back. Their devotion to the young company did not end there.

"We were desperately trying to keep our noses above water and sell whatever we could," Dick recalled.

The early crew hardly ever went out to lunch. At the same time, they still enjoyed and sometimes relished the lunchtime. "We would have a good time while throwing out ideas and joking," Mary Nell said. "None of us wanted to go out. The phone was always ringing with orders or requests or to develop something for an account." Part of their dedication came from Dick's and Jinnie's fascination for the whole new process. Here they were building a business that they had conceived. They could have gone into big companies if they had wanted to, but neither had chosen that.

Dick quit playing golf the day the company started. It was quite a change because before that time, he played three or four times a week.

"I learned much from them," Mary Nell said. "Part of that was learning fair and honest business practices. They had principles that were rare in most businesses. They were totally fair. That involved the way they dealt with not just customers, but with the few sales people they had."

The decade would end on a sad and solemn note for Dick and Jinnie when their son, Rick, was attending the Mills School in Ft. Lauderdale, Fla., the closest good one of its kind for children with dyslexia. He was a good swimmer, but he drowned in 1969, the second year he attended there. The loss of their son was a profound one, yet, together they continued to build the company. There would be many growth and stretch challenges for both the company and the family as the seventies decade dawned.

III

Trailblazing Through the 1970s

THE 1970S WOULD MARK THE START OF A DECADE IN which the company began to make great strides with diversification of its main product lines and started doing specialty work for notable customers, such as Honeywell, the U.S. Department of Agriculture, Skylab and the NASA space programs.

The decade also marked the milestone of the company building its first fluorescent emergency ballast. David Crippen had the difficult job of selling a new and unique product few people had ever heard of. He proved to be successful after a lot of effort and the Bodine Co. built layer on layer of earned market awareness as an innovative company with superior customer service. From that point onward, untold lives literally have depended on the quality of the products that the Bodine Co. shipped out of its doors.

Over time, the innovative *Tran*-BAL® experienced widespread applications – mostly customer-driven. These include vehicle lighting in ambulances, buses, commercial vans and subways; as well as flicker-free light sources for photoelectric applications, inspection systems, scanning equipment, reprographic equipment and more.

Product development was not the only challenge. "Early after the move into the facility in Collierville when we had grown to 10 or 12 employees, we began to get (internal) reports of hostility or conflict about two people not getting along," Dick recalled.

Jinnie using her power of social and business persuasion.

There were some racial subtexts to the concerns or discussions. That is when Jinnie got all of the employees to meet in an empty office. They sat around on the floor in that office and started talking about how accusations were going around about how one person felt on one side or the other.

Jinnie said, "OK, you are saying...so and so is doing or thinking this. How do you know?"

The person being questioned said, "I can tell by looking at her."

"You can read her mind?" Jinnie asked. She then listened to what everyone had to say. It must have taken an hour or more. For the first time, the group entered into broader group thinking and they ultimately admitted they didn't really know what the other person was thinking.

"Ever since that session, we never have had racial conflicts at our company," Dick said proudly. "We saw real compatibility and harmony from then on." Indeed, Jinnie had an uncanny way of reading people. When she interviewed Al Lyons for a job there to replace his banking position he had held elsewhere, she spent a couple of hours talking with him about psychology, an area he had studied in addition to finance and accounting.

"When I got home, I felt certain I didn't have the job and years later, I asked her why she had focused on that topic," Al said. "She told me, 'Al, I knew you knew about accounting. I wanted to see what you knew about psychology, an important part of any business.' What she taught me is that you can look at the numbers, but you have to temper that by your feelings. Make a decision based on that combination and it makes for good business. She certainly used both sides of the brain." Al would rise to the ranks of president of the company over time, retiring in February 2008 after almost 34 years at Bodine.

Occasionally, there were periods of business doldrums. The management was committed, though, to no layoffs. Sometimes, employees were given buckets of paint and were told to paint building walls. Being skilled at playing ping-pong was considered to be an asset during these business downturns as well. Most of all, the employees were treated like a big family.

Everyone has to take vacations, though. In 1971, Dick and Jinnie celebrated their 25th wedding anniversary with a trip to St. Thomas and a side trip to St. John, where they were given

Our first building. It took us a couple of years to get enough money to pave the parking lot. One day. a woman noticed the logo and asked if we made birth control compounds.

snorkels, masks and fins to see the underwater nature park. "We could hardly wait to get home and take scuba diving lessons so we could really get down there with the lovely coral and fish," Jinnie recalled in her 1995 letter. "After that, we spent our vacations diving all over the Caribbean and playing tennis on some of the strangest courts – with fishnet for backstops!"

Vacations aside, the business continued making very bold steps of its own. The mid-1970s yielded another milestone when *TranBAL®* DC inverter ballasts were used as part of an experiment on NASA's SkyLab space station. Skylab was the first space station the United States launched into orbit and the second space station ever visited by a human crew. The 100-ton space station was in Earth's orbit from 1973 to 1979 and it was visited by crews three times in 1973 and 1974. It included a laboratory for studying the effects of micro gravity and an Apollo telescope-mount solar observatory.

The Bodine Co. also put out its first newsletter, The Bodine Bulletin, in 1977 right before Christmas. That noted that it had just chalked up the largest order the company had yet received – hundreds of *Tran*-BAL® units. This order was broadcast for delivery, and presumably payment, over a period of about half a year. The company was going gangbusters at that time with average sales of about 1,300 B-50 units each month. The B-50 version of the core unit was and still is one of Bodine's most important emergency ballasts. B-50s also were the first "officially" named fluorescent emergency ballasts, and for many years, were the singular emergency ballast product. Later on came the B-70, B-90, and a host of others, but the B-50 was the granddaddy of the fluorescent emergency ballast line.

There were a couple of other interesting applications of Bodine products in the 1970s. One was for a potato sorting machine. In the machine, the potatoes were fed into a pump that blew them past viewing chambers. A fluorescent light sorted out the bad potatoes from the good ones for this manufacturing process. Inside this viewing chamber was Bodine's own *Tran*-BAL®, acting as the light source for that machine made by the Electric Sorting Machine Division of Geosource Inc. of Houston.

In another specialty application, a customer in Louisville, Colo., Storage Technology, was involved in magnetic storage devices for computers. For this Western account, Bodine devised part of the backup systems for its disc drives. The magnetic tapes in these devices would come off the reels and go through a set of driver pulleys, looping down to the bottom, then back up onto another wheel. The drive wheels could reverse the tapes quickly, but could not stop the take-up wheels at the correct intervals. The Bodine Co. provided a fluorescent light that used photo cells to monitor motion so that the last photo cell to "see" the tape registered that the end of the tape was on the reel-to-reel tapes.

It kept the operators from having broken spools. The sensors further would direct the variance of tape. A *Tran*-BAL® powered the fluorescent tube for the optical limit switch inside these data mechanisms. Data for computers in former times were kept on magnetic tape since there was not widespread solid state memory that is available now.

In 1978, a director from the Mining Enforcement and Safety Administration made DC fluorescent lighting mandatory. The Bodine Co. was involved in the development, meanwhile, of a high-voltage (128V) DC ballast to operate the needed high-output fluorescent lamps. The company was the first to develop the *Tran*-BAL® inverter ballast necessary to operate this type of underground lighting.

And 150 miles west of Tucson, Arizona, the residential villages of a small Native American group were the setting for a NASA test of solar lighting systems to provide their first artificial lighting. This was made possible by the development of an electronic ballast that operates a fluorescent lamp from a DC source. That ballast was developed by the company. The power station consisted of batteries charged by solar energy during daylight hours to provide power for lights at night. The whole venture got started because the reservation was so remote that it wasn't placed on a conventional electrical power grid, Al Lyons explained.

These were made-to-order situations that Dick loved. As a classic entrepreneur in the purest sense, he wasn't interested in buying outside solutions or even components, Bodine engineering manager Alex Ertz mused years later. Alex later served as general manager of the company.

"Bodine Co. was always extremely vertically integrated and thus, interlinked among the facets needed for production," Alex said. "We even painted the cases of our products and put together the circuit boards. Dick always wanted to do things in-house. He would say, 'I can do that,' down to his creating his own processing

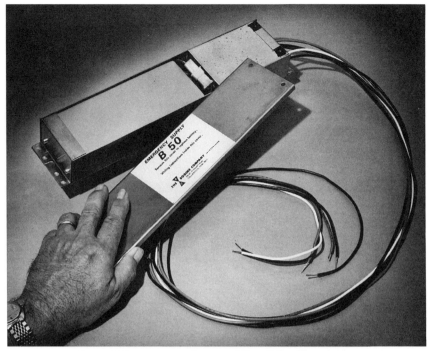

One of the most poplar models of the fluorescent emergency ballasts, the B50.

programs that probably could have been sold commercially when he finished with them."

Rather than being cheap, Alex said Dick thrived on the intellectual challenge and thought he could "do it better!" Those are signs of the true entrepreneur.

Ping pong was such an avid pursuit at the company that it was almost part of the line of questions at job interviews, although not formally. Suffice to say, it was played almost every break by someone, even after a full day of work.

"Once, we were missing multiple ping pong balls," Al said. "Back, then, there was no place in Collierville to buy these balls. We had to order them from a Sears outlet or bring them from Memphis. We noticed that several were missing and went on a hunt. More balls started disappearing. This went on for several weeks. Then we went into the R&D lab and saw several ping

Jinnie busily going over a detailed report in her office.

pong balls cut in half. Dick had needed a lens cap over a photo cell, so he was taking these and using them for this improvised purpose."

The output during the 1970s increased at such a rate that the company began an in-depth study of the cost of materials used. This was accomplished by the purchasing department becoming more aggressive in getting the best prices. In time, Bodine became a big enough customer to the extent that some of the needed supplies were on consignment. It permitted the company to coordinate the estimated needs of the sales and production departments to make sure necessary materials were always available to fill orders.

Dick learned how to use and program computers during this decade. His first computer was just a little circuit board. To program it, Dick had to enter each entry by itself. If any mistakes were made, he'd have to start all over.

The company heard some presentations and was initially put off by IBM, thanks to a meeting in which the IBM salesmen soured themselves, Al said. "IBM came in to make a presentation and took a look at our computer systems. The first thing they did when they came into our conference room was to demand to know about every aspect of our company before they would make any specifications. They should have done some of that work before they came here. Dick was PO'd at that and pretty much shut down the meeting. He wrote IBM off because of their big-guy, presumptuous attitude."

Exterior of the original building

Then the company bought a Wang with an IBM disk drive. It had a 5 megabyte removable disk. When using the Wang word processing system Dick had designed, the user was limited to 50 lines of type on one page and the program lacked the many features that today's word processing systems boast. Nonetheless, employees who became computer-literate on Dick's computer system were well-equipped to embrace the bigger wave of all-pervasive business computer use that swept in during the late 1980s and early 1990s.

To get accustomed to the system, Bodine staff members were encouraged by the installers to play Star Wars games during lunch. "They were playing Star Wars one time and the computer system got stuck," Al recalled. "So we turned them off to reboot them. It turned out that Jinnie was running payroll, so that caused a bit of a ruckus."

Sometimes, small mistakes also caused momentary angst. "When I was first hired, one of the first things I noticed was that the menu entry for "Miscellaneous" was spelled wrong," Beth Hoople recalled. "Because Dick was the entire information technology department back then, he was the only person I could point out the mistake to. Tell the head honcho about his mistake? I approached the task with fear and trepidation. But like everything else, Dick made it clear that he hired other people to be experts in what he was not good at himself and that included some details about spelling and grammar. He thanked me, corrected the error, and made it clear he expected any other mistakes to be pointed out to maintain the quality reputation of his company."

The Bodine Co. input job cards into its computer daily, even back in the 1970s. That was so the computer could keep up with an average time for each process. When a customer placed a large *Tran*-BAL® order, it was impossible to give them a correct price per unit. Jim Cagle would write down the job process numbers and Al would supply the parts lists. These were then fed into the computer, which figured the time and cost to build the order. All of this included labor, materials and setup time. It also revealed how much gross profit would be made on each unit. This was considered pretty sophisticated for its time.

Until then, Jinnie had to set the prices by asking Jim or Dick, "How long will it take to build them and how much should we charge?" If the three of them guessed incorrectly, they either would lose the job or lose money building the units.

Longtime employee Connie Wilson started working in the print shop at Bodine in 1977. Her mom had worked at Sears in Collierville and Jim Cagle visited that store often. Connie's mom asked Jim one day whether Bodine was hiring. He told her they needed someone to work in the print shop. "Although I knew nothing about printing, I came in to interview with George Bust-

A pondering moment of Dick's in his work lab.

eed, the graphic artist manager at that time." It was a successful meeting for Connie and she was hired. (George also was one of the founders of the In-Plant Printers Management Association in Memphis, an organization for in-house printers to share information on vendors selling paper, ink and other supplies for the printing industry).

Connie vividly recalled one fiscal year-end in March 1977 when Dick and Jinnie opened a bottle of champagne to celebrate the first million-dollar year. "I received my first bonus check after only working here three months and thought that it was great that they believed in their employees enough to share in the profits of the company," she said. "It was family-owned and they treated us like part of the family. Dick and Jinnie only took two weeks' vacation like everyone else the whole time they worked. They were here late most every night. I thought they could do anything they wanted because they owned the place, but they were devoted to working."

About 25 to 30 people were working at the Bodine Co. when Connie started. "I thought to myself, 'How many emergency lights can people possibly want?' I mean, once we made some and shipped them out, I thought we would supply most of the need and not grow much more than a million dollars per year for a long time to come," she said. "Not true! As we did start to grow, even though we had slow months when there was not much building going on, I remember Dick and Jinnie had us paint or clean baseboards or windows. Most of us wore many hats. They believed in teamwork. I watched as the company kept growing and concluded we were strong because of the foundation built by Dick and Jinnie."

Connie also noticed how modestly the Bodines lived and that it was the end of the 1970s before they had central air installed in their Germantown home.

This is a view of a production area within the
Collierville plant in the late 1970s/early 1980s.

As the company became more sophisticated, the advertising department started taking a larger role. Tech-Nik Advertising, as it was called, was operated as a separate division with its own annual budget. Included in it were all ads and promotions for each product line, printing facilities and personnel. The Bodines decided to maintain these in-house capabilities because Bodine could do the job less expensively and with better control over quality and security. In a four-year span in the 1970s, it went from two cartons of paper inventory to about 100 cartons that were constantly moving through its Tech-Nik print shop. Starting out with a small one-color press, it grew during the decade into an equipped press room with a two-color press. This in-plant print shop produced stunning published materials during its heyday. Usually, printing four-color brochures demanded a four-color press. To produce a four-color job, they would run the same pieces of paper through the two-color press twice — a real challenge, since registration for just one run through the press demanded a high degree of expertise. Going through twice made it twice as hard. And several times, the Marketing Department challenged the graphic artist and printing experts to add a fifth color and varnish overlay. Several hundred thousand pieces of paper were fed through the two-color press three times, with remarkably professional results — to the astonishment of other local printing experts.

The letterhead that was used for all the Bodine Co's. correspondence for years expressed their faith ethic at the bottom. "To know and feel the presence of God is the most exhilarating experience known to man." While it received critical comments from some outside the company, these were few in number. What really shook the Bodines up years later, though, was for someone to finally point out that they had misspelled the word, "exhilarating." When they retired, the slogan was phased out of the stationery. Their faith at work seldom took the form of preaching or quoting Bible verses, though. It was more like a pervasive feeling that this was a place where good — good works, good feelings, good products, good times — were embraced. Evil, in whatever form, was something to avoid and to work hard to eliminate from everyday life.

☙

IV

Success Attained: the Decade of the 1980s

THE DECADE OF THE 1980S STARTED WITH DICK undergoing a heart bypass operation. He had not had a heart attack, but suffered complications from the closing of arteries, caused mostly by cholesterol buildup. Stress tests had revealed some were blocked. The surgery required a quintuple bypass procedure. After the operation, both he and Jinnie changed their diets drastically.

"After surgery, we changed our diets to eliminate as much of the foods high in fat content that we could – basically what is now called heart-friendly," Dick said. Not only that, but when he woke up each morning before the break of day, Dick would walk five miles. He did that for years.

Employees who had traditionally sat at the same lunch table with Dick whispered among themselves that the heart problems must have been caused by his daily diet of pimiento cheese sandwiches and bags of Fritos.

"Because we were still a small company, we pitched in together and rented a belly dancer for Dick's return," Connie recalled. The whole company gathered in the front lobby, hid the belly dancer in the conference room and asked Dick to come out of his office because they wanted to welcome him back to work.

"Well, when the music started, it was loud, and we opened the door to the conference room, and out comes the dancer," Connie said. "I thought I was going to have a heart attack; I thought,

Dick on the phone in the 1970s in a Collierville office, papers askew, showing the seamless activity.

'Oh no, we're going to put this man back in the hospital.' Nevertheless, he handled it very well."

The new athletic regimen served him well because years later, when a hip replacement became necessary, Dick underwent more tests that revealed the arteries were clear.

It's not as if the Bodines weren't already an active couple. To varying degrees, they still shared their mutual interests in scuba diving and tennis. Their favorite spot became Little Dix Bay Resort on Virgin Gorda, one of the British Virgin Islands. There were no TV sets or phones to distract and even the rooms didn't have locks on the doors. It was just a perfect island hideaway.

"When we started scuba diving, we'd pick out a place off the beaten path where it was really hard to get in touch with us," Dick remembered. "Jinnie would get the managers of our different departments together before we left town and select one to be the 'last word' so that in turn, each one would have that (chain of) responsibility. Their instructions were to not call us unless someone died and not to leave any decisions for us. If they could not reach a consensus, the 'Last Word' had to make it. This proved to be good training for the management. As an added benefit, we didn't have to spend our vacations worrying about what was going on."

Vertical integration (consolidation of component materials to retain more of the work processes in-house) was expanded. It also came in the form of a purchase of the company's chief wire supplier in 1982, extending that further after its acquisition. This line would, over the decade, gain a reputation in its own right. It grew into a large, highly efficient operation. Bodine's wire workers are able to cut, dye or terminate a variety of wire or to design efficient wire harnesses to meet specific needs. At that stage, maintaining profitability in the wire business was a tremendous challenge because small "mom-and-pop" businesses were producing similar products at highly competitive prices. But these small businesses could not maintain the quality as they increased volume. Yet, Bodine could.

The company was gaining momentum by the month. Jinnie wrote in a newsletter in the early 1980s: "While business has continued to be good all along, incoming orders have increased at an astonishing rate. While the rest of the country seems to be shutting down, Bodine is going stronger than ever."

An interesting application for Kodak used a photo cell and fluorescent light to measure the thickness of the emulsions applied to film. The problem was that light from fluorescent lights would flicker on and off at twice the frequency of what was driving the lamp itself. It made the system sense the emulsion was going on thicker or thinner than it actually was. This was a production problem that had no effect on the consumer. However, unless the emulsion was even in the production cycle, the film was rated as faulty and not used.

"We designed a *Tran*-BAL® that ran the light at such a high frequency that the variations were not noticeable by the film depositing system," Dick said. "We grew to have specialized systems like that."

With the company having grown to 72 employees, Dick worked on the business' first corporate computer system. Dick and Jinnie also agreed with David Crippen that it was time to hire someone to handle business communications. Although they had only a rough idea of what the position would entail. In 1983, they advertised for and hired Beth Hoople.

"At that time," Beth said, "those types of jobs still were more common in mega-companies. Small or mid-sized companies rarely had the computer technology that Dick had developed. Additionally, they had an in-plant print shop, which was also a rarity except in huge corporations.

"When I stepped into the job, the duties were sketchy and ill-defined. But the situation was a perfect fit because they understood the importance of communications. I was able to create the job, and with some excellent teamwork, develop a mini 'publishing empire.' Everyone there had to be creative, wear a lot of hats, be adaptable to change, and be ready to promote a product that Dick and his team of engineers developed during an 'Aha!' moment."

Eventually, the sales and engineering team, with the help of a graphic artist and in-house print shop miracle-workers, expanded newsletter and print advertising substantially. A monthly newsletter to employees and manufacturers' representatives maintained a constant barrage of news and product promotions. Every-other-month newsletters to lighting fixture manufacturers, who represented a major slice of the sales pie, kept Bodine quality and innovation in front of buying decision-makers. And quarterly missives to contractor-installers and lighting architectural engineers promoted specification-grade products and services.

It was this public relations machine that helped put into motion the triumph of the 1984 Business of the Year award. That year, the Bodine Co. was feted in a banquet as the Business of the Year in the 26-100 employee category for the 1983 Small Business Awards. The firm was chosen by judges for its age-old business principles of ingenuity.

The company description, outlined on the evening of the awards, read: "Bodine is a high-tech company that blends well with the tree-covered lanes of the old part of Collierville. It is devoted to the manufacture of inverter ballasts for lighting fixtures, invisible emergency lighting packs for schools and factories and research and development for other products." About 1,000 attended the awards banquet at The Peabody hotel.

Upon receiving the award, Dick offered an old-fashioned philosophy: "Don't buy it until you can pay for it."

As the 1980s continued, Bodine Co. continued to grow. In the mid-decade, West Coast customers, motivated by power failures, bought Bodine equipment. The Bodine sales agent in Seattle reported several power shortages, including one that affected a large part of the city. Many citizens were caught short without emergency lighting and the fire marshal was kept busy making sure businesses were in compliance with local codes. The company sold more in that area because of this concern. Although there were not reports of fines being levied for noncompliance, several customers mentioned having to prove they had met codes by a certain deadline.

Building owners and managers weren't concerned about cost as much as they were about a long-term solution. A salesman was able to sell B50 models on the strength of a five-year warranty. These customers wanted a product that would ensure they wouldn't have the same problem with the fire marshal in a year or two. After every major domestic hurricane, power blackout or devastating storm, sales of fluorescent emergency ballasts to the affected city made a brief but noticeable jump.

Another kind of catastrophe brought another sale. The day after the Six-Day War broke out in Israel, an order for 72 fluorescent emergency ballasts came through for shipment to Tel Aviv.

David Crippen had long instituted a regimen among the sales force to make presentations on emergency lighting and other systems to all lighting engineers, electrical engineers and architects in their territories. He always said, "Product awareness is the first stage of the buying process." The premise was that if the lighting specification community was not aware of the products, they could not specify them. He would invite hard questions from the sales team as they made more people aware of the technology. He also wanted to learn ways the products could be improved, along with reactions from specifiers during presentations.

By this decade, the Bodine Co. had gained more of a stronghold in the industry. As a result of a series of meetings to further the company's corporate strategy, it became able to tout things most other manufacturers could not. Part of that was its ability to take long-term looks at each product line and the company as a whole. Bodine's products in particular became known for the following:

- Lower input power generated less heat, extending the life of the components and batteries
- A higher battery capacity, meaning more power could be stored so more lighting source was available when needed
- Batteries with a few large cells rather than a lot of small cells, averted failures
- Fewer parts on the circuitry, promoting reliability
- A smaller case than competitors' models, allowing for wiring in the ballast channel
- More varieties of wattages and types of lamps because of the efficiency of its inverter circuit design. That also helped eliminate compatibility problems.

In addition, customers soon favored fluorescent over incandescent exit illumination in general because fluorescents have longer life spans and there is less re-lamping time with fluorescents, lowering maintenance costs.

Moreover, employee benefits began to become a drawing card and Bodine was innovative in that it would underwrite employees' college courses, including tuition and books. The only requirements were that they had to have worked full time for the company for one year, the courses should relate to the company's business, and the employee had to pass any courses they were enrolled to take.

With ramped-up production and additional employees coming on board, the campus build-out started to occur. Jinnie once kidded that, "We realized that we've been using the wrong signals for deciding when to add on. Rather than waiting until it's too crowded to move in the production

David Crippen in a casual pose soon after he started working for the company.

area, from now on, the signal for when to start construction will be when we have to take down the ping-pong table!"

One who would spearhead much of the company's engineering impetus from the early 1980s to the present was Alex Ertz, who had excelled at Christian Brothers University and then through installing electronics systems for Caterpillar. It was when he joined Bodine, though, that he knew he had found his true haven.

"Memphis was not a hotbed of electronic innovation, so this was just the kind of rare environment I was seeking," said Alex, who, like Dick, always tinkered with electrical systems and said that even as a teenager, he had Popular Mechanics books and wiring all over his bedroom.

There was not a lot of attention paid to patenting each applicable device the company would turn out until Dick met a patent attorney from Los Angeles while they were on a trip in the Caribbean, Alex recalled. "We learned of the importance of applying patent protection on the work we did on energy management systems in the early- to mid-1980s," Alex said. "We studied intellectual property on that for the high-intensity discharge emergency lamps I was working on. Dick did have a patent on the high-pressure sodium lamp igniters and another project, at least." Meanwhile, the *Tran-BAL®* didn't have a patent itself, with Dick having the attitude that he didn't invent it stem to stern but created its industry applications.

To augment the service to customers in the mid-1980s, the company instituted a full lineup of customer support programs. These included a toll-free number, direct factory contacts for field problems, technical assistance, wiring diagrams for applications, and a newsletter. In addition, its production quality backed it up. Its defective rate then was less than a tenth of 1 percent, but if a customer received a ballast that didn't work, the factory would return a new unit.

In addition, the marketing team, still headed by David Crippen, implemented another "special" feature that other manufacturers didn't have. A little research showed that painting the ballast boxes red, instead of black, further distinguished Bodine fluorescent emergency ballasts from all others on the market. The phrase "If it's red, it's Bodine" was churned into the advertising mix and customers would know a red emergency ballast meant top-of-the-line power-outage protection.

David was attending an NFPA (National Fire Protection Association) meeting once and asked a fire extinguisher engineer why fire extinguishers were red and yellow. The engineer said, "They differentiate one type from another." David said Bodine was sometimes confused with standard AC ballasts and the color gave the company a chance to promote the "emergency" or life-safety aspects of its products.

"Dick's whole thing was to innovate and David's was to sell, sell," Alex said. Innovation was not only occurring out in the field. In 1986, the company installed a bobbin-soldering robot in the production area. After much experimentation, the production engineers got the robot to dip bobbins all day long.

Other specialists would come into the fold to help company management innovate. In 1985, Brad Van Frank was six months out of college and preparing to go to Kansas City to interview as a graphic artist at Hallmark's headquarters.

What stopped him in his route was an ad he spotted for a graphic designer in his hometown. Bodine was seeking such a person to join its team. He interviewed with the print shop manager and was hired to expand the company's advertising promotions. For someone who had an interim job in a hardware store and who wanted to remain in his hometown, Brad welcomed the opportunity.

By 1987, Bodine's R&D engineers worked with a then-sophisticated HP computer system capable of generating prototype models. The models were computer tested so early bugs could be worked out first. Two employees were engaged in computer-aided design (CAD) system drafting and also used a plotter to produce drawings and diagrams. No computer system, though, replaced the grinding, day-after-day testing, checking and rechecking of parts and finished products. Every batch of products was tested to make sure they worked before being used in production. Even the transformers were wound at R&D to make sure they met specifications. Batteries would undergo a whole series of quality checks such as charging and discharging. Then they were subjected to high-temperature tests to measure their capacity at certain temperatures.

On the production line, 11 critical functions were tested before products were boxed and records were kept of those tests. After the boxes were packed into cartons, a percentage of the day's production was pulled and checked to make sure the installation, instruction, parts and labels were correct.

*A scene in the plant showing one of the machines used
to cut and terminate wires for component use.*

During the same decade, the company hired many of its other long-time employees who are there to this day. Dick hired a young computer programmer to help him rewrite the company's computer software when it made the switch from Wang to Digital brand computers. The Wang computer was designed primarily for word processing while the Digital was more of a general-use computer. The Digital was more powerful and faster and could handle more users. Back then, there were not computer interface packages to bridge the two automatically. It was a very laborious effort with few interchangeable and universal programs. Moreover, one could not simply put in a floppy disk, CD rom or flash drive with 1 GB of memory to move data from one to the other. "We worked side by side for a couple of years doing this," Dick said.

Dick's inventive mind was not to be underestimated. Alex told a tale of something Dick tried to devise during the 1980s that

Swiss labs are working to perfect even today through the use of Blue Tooth technology.

"Dick always would be thinking of creating things," Alex said. "Before the days of programmable thermostats, he wanted to have a deal where over the phone line, he could remotely control them. He built a telephone remote control that could turn things on and off through the touch-tone phones.

"This encoding was accomplished before anything was done with micro-processing and it was over regular phone lines. He was able to remotely turn things on and off in the house and he was happy with that one application and didn't even try to duplicate it." Jinnie and Dick used this device in their home on Dogwood to control the lights and the heat when they left for work.

Like an electronics version of Jules Verne, Dick Bodine was all on top of that a quarter of a century earlier. Only the components had not been invented yet.

(At the Haute Ecole Technical University in Sion, Switzerland, scientists in 2007 were developing embedded systems and wireless technology to send programs through remote control manipulation. One recent test used a cell phone as a remote control, much as a joy stick, to create a telephone interface for any electronic device. It uses Blue Tooth PDA and touch screens with the device, sending its control programs through any Blue Tooth device. At this juncture, the scientists are studying processor power and memory usage. They are using Universal Modeling Language (UML) code and basically marrying the functions of wireless telecommunications with computing. They say it may soon be possible, for instance, to communicate with guests who are en route to your home and then distantly open a garage door for them or unlock doors just in time for their arrival via cell phone technology).

As a subcontractor, the Bodine Co. once was asked to bid on a design-build project involving a special light to go onto a rescue

A midpoint assembly line point.

submarine called the DSRV (Deep Submersible Rescue Vehicle). It took an engineer two years to design the light and the company quoted the U.S. government $99,000 for the first one. The government thought that was a bargain. After that first one was accepted, the company received orders for 32 of them. The specs required that the devices be able to withstand pressures five miles deep into the ocean. They were housed in titanium with half-inch thick walls, Dick recalled. Production versions went for about $3,500 each to the government.

All the while, the company was paying attention to building up its staff. Lamar Brock joined the company in the late 1980s, filling the job of human resources director. "I remember it well because for our retirement party, we rented the Memphis Queen riverboat and had a big party," Lamar said. They had ordered customized L.L. Bean jackets for every Bodine employee with their names on each.

Because Lamar had just been hired, there wasn't a jacket for him yet. However, there was one jacket left with no one's name on it and Jinnie gave that one to him. Lamar's mission, he said of his new job, was to communicate, to motivate and train.

Controller Robert Young had a humorous memory of Lamar and others when he joined the enterprise in 1989 as a plant accountant. It was easy to remember people then, because there were still less than 100 employees. "My first day here it was such a relaxed environment; there were guys wearing blue jeans and Lamar, the HR manager, was wearing all black. I thought, 'Where in the world am I? It was a different environment and one I have grown to love. The atmosphere has always been a pleasant working environment. It is a unique place with openness. It's different from any place I have seen."

Parties were regular occasions at this family company. Dick and Jinnie would not only set party dates for regular events on the calendar, but also for attaining significant achievements or for launching a new product.

These parties took the form of Christmas gatherings, Easter egg hunts, the spring Picnic, Halloween costume parties and revenue milestone celebrations. And Thanksgiving was not just something folks observed at home. They celebrated at the company first with a potluck buffet. It was a good complement to the summer picnic, which was a popular outdoor event with good food, volleyball, horseshoes, and yes, ping-pong.

At the quarter-century mark party of 1987 on a river boat, Dick and Jinnie received a silver emergency ballast and silver quartz clock. Graphics department leader Brad Van Frank said, "They allowed the employees to celebrate with them."

When Brad started working at the company, he became involved in helping put the Bodine name out there boldly across the emergency fluorescent market to further develop brand equity for the business. "Many of our early advertising campaigns were an attempt to teach the specifiers what emergency lighting was," he said. "We were really introducing a new concept and we did that for many years, trying to establish the market."

The red color of the cases played a big part in that brand identity and recognition. "It tied us in with the whole life safety market," Brad said. "We since have continued to be very flexible in providing solutions for our customers. We are now the Burger King of emergency lights because we provide our customers with just about anything they want in terms of applications."

A Bodine Co. model called the HID 1600 was one of the forerunners in this spectrum of products. One of these was specified for use in a school gym in Nebraska and a second early one sold to Metropolitan Edison, the giant power company. Meanwhile, the tried and trusted B-50s were being sold to places as far away as Saudi Arabia. They had to have special labels indicating they were made in the U.S.A., a rule required by the Saudi Arabian Standards Organization. Meanwhile, another then-new emergency ballast, the B-90, was modified for a Seiko plant in Yokohama, Japan.

In addition, a *Tran*-BAL® played a large part in transmitting photographs of the 1988 Olympics in Calgary to a newspaper in Springfield, Mass. The equipment was part of a Leafax 35 scanner-transmitter that could transmit a photo image of a film negative to a laser camera that recorded a photo ready to be used by the newspaper. That eliminated the need for a photographer to develop negatives into a photograph before it could be used. The briefcase-sized Leafax 35 used a *Tran*-BAL® to illuminate a fluorescent lamp and provide a way for news photographers to spend less time in the darkroom and more time taking pictures.

Production manager Gregg Mosley, who had started with the Bodine Co. about a decade earlier, sees a major milestone as tied to the very one unearthed in its formative years. "It was getting our type of emergency ballast to operate on two D cells, which we'd been working on for a time," he said. "The way we approached it was to use a voltage multiplier and operate a fluorescent lamp on a DC rather than AC voltage. For years after that, the industry went to that mode."

DC is a steady state voltage that can be used for many of the same things as AC, such as lighting a light bulb. The big drawback is the inability to change the voltage easily. By using transformers, AC can be easily changed to whatever is needed. The Bodine units operated from DC, but the circuits inside converted current to AC. In almost anything electronic, both will be used in various parts of the circuit. DC voltage does not change polarity, while AC does.

Gregg, who retired in 2008, oversaw the layout of the production lines and was responsible for incoming inspection of parts and other production needs. He was the one person authorized to shut down production with no one second-guessing him. Gregg had long had an uncanny ability to detect bad parts when they were unloaded off the truck and unpackaged. It is alleged that his ears would tingle when a bad part was delivered to the Bodine Co. Generally soft-spoken and taciturn, he also has the ability to deliver a verbal "zinger" to generate a round of hearty laughter.

Laughter has long been a common denominator at the Bodine Co. In his early days of working with the company, Gregg was summoned to Dick's office. Full of natural apprehension, his mind racing as he walked down the hall, he was amazed when Dick whipped out a bunny rabbit suit and asked him to wear it for the company's annual Easter egg party. Summoning his courage, he responded with a flat "No, I won't do that." Years later, Dick would kid Gregg about not dressing up for that occasion.

Gregg will always be indebted to the company, though, for many reasons. In the early 1980s, he had to go into the hospital for back surgery. Dick recommended a surgeon from Campbell Clinic. Gregg had to be out of commission for six to eight weeks and was fearful that his pay would be docked for exceeding the annual leave limits. "Strangely, I didn't miss a paycheck and I was grateful," he said.

Gregg recalled that Dick would visit the company's labs even when he wasn't inventing something himself. He didn't micro-manage, but he always wanted to be up on things. "I always had two projects that I was working on," Gregg said. "There was the one he wanted me to be working on and the one I thought I should be working on. I had to shift back and forth to the projects, depending on when he would visit the workroom."

David Crippen recently reflected on the legacy that Dick and Jinnie left the company and to him in particular.

"I have the utmost respect for Dick and Jinnie Bodine," he said. "I learned so much from them about dealing with people. They were fair and firm. Their paternalistic management style worked very well. Another amazing thing is that they worked all day together and then went home to spend the evening and night together. I cannot recall one instance where they came to work angry with each other over something that happened at home."

David also vividly recalls a conversation he had with Dick when the boss once asked him, "How can we sell more?"

David replied, "You need to make our products smaller so they could more easily be installed in the fluorescent fixtures."

Dick retorted, "I can't make them smaller."

David replied, "I can't sell more."

Dick then went back to the lab and worked for several months, finally succeeding in devising a smaller product. The Bodine Co. sold tens of thousands of them.

It was on a vacation trip to the Caribbean in 1988 that Dick and Jinnie did some big turn-of-life thinking. "I began to think of those two pieces of paper in the bank safety deposit box, our stock certificates in the company," she recalled in the 1995 letter. "We couldn't eat them or play with them and they didn't do anything but sit there. Why not convert them to something we could enjoy, like money? We had contributed about all we could to the company. Some of our managers needed new challenges to be on their own."

On an otherwise quiet Tuesday afternoon, Dick and Jinnie requested all employees attend a short meeting in the lunchroom. Dick took the floor and said, "We counted up our bumps and bruises and decided that we need to retire before our wheelchairs don't roll anymore."

When Dick and Jinnie retired in 1988, they turned down several offers from outsiders and instead sold the company to the employees in a tailored form of leveraged buyout that used an Employee Stock Ownership Plan. Financing their loyal employees' purchase of the company was Dick and Jinnie's prime example of generosity toward their coworkers. The transaction called for selling the company to the people they most wanted to assume ownership – the employees themselves. As written, the plan permitted the Bodines to make it easy for the employees to pay them over a 15-year period. There were about 115 employees when the couple retired.

Investing financially in the employees was not a new occurrence, and acted as a prototype, in a sense, years before the plan was determined for the company to become employee-owned.

"Dick and Jinnie cared greatly for whatever they were involved in, including the Bodine School," Connie said. "They also cared about the employees of the company. When I started working at Bodine in the 1970s, Jinnie had told me about the profit sharing plan. I was too young at the time to be fully into it — I believe the law then said you had to be 24 and a half to join. As I became older and fully vested, I thought again that I was so blessed to be working for Bodine. When you are young, you don't think about getting old. Jinnie always talked to us when she passed out the profit sharing statement or the end-of-the year bonus checks of how important it is to save or invest."

Dick's and Jinnie's retirement was a sad event for many of the employees, but even their farewell party at the company was low-key and focused on the business, its successes and its people rather than on the hard-working founders.

"When we sold the company to the employees, Jinnie set it up like this," Dick said. "She had previously set up an employee stock ownership plan (ESOP) that held 30 percent of the stock. She increased its percentage to 49%. The other 51% was then bought by a group of employees, which gave them control. As time went on, several of them retired and left Al Lyon, David Crippen and Alex Ertz with the remainder of the stock." By mutual consent, part of the sales agreement precluded Jinnie or Dick from retaining any stock in the company.

Dick thought initially it might be difficult to retire, but the first morning the alarm clock didn't ring, he was convinced. Neither he nor Jinnie had a single regret of doing so afterward. The Bodines also decided to take up golf again. Neither had played golf since they started the company. They just didn't have the time. They had heard that St. Croix had an excellent golf course, so they tried it. They found everyone there to be friendly and laid-back. It was like living 60 years back in time, Jinnie felt. A few months later, they returned for a week, decided on a property the moment they saw it, bought it and selected an architect and a contractor. "The morning we were to leave, the architects presented sketches of what he thought we wanted," Jinnie said. "It was. We said, 'Do it!'"

Jinnie Bodine

Unfortunately, it took a long time to draw up the plans and order the materials. When Hurricane Hugo demolished the island in September 1989, only the excavation was completed. All the Bodines lost, though, was about six months of time. When it was completed, they loved the remote, but comfortable residence. It sports a 9-foot-wide covered porch all around and many windows and doors, which are always open with no need for heating or air conditioning.

Soon, the Bodines became interested in many of the island activities such as the Boys and Girls Club, the Queen Louise Home for Children, the rebuilding of a hospital destroyed by Hugo, and other pursuits.

"We have fallen so in love with this island and the people, that we have moved our residency here and only go back to Memphis for a few weeks in May and October and for special events," Jinnie once wrote in a letter to a friend.

For a few years after Jinnie retired and before the couple moved into the home on the Caribbean island, she established a healthy-style eatery on Sanderlin near the Racquet Club of Memphis. Called Dinners a la Heart, its fare was based on health-wise recipes. It sold food that was low-cholesterol, low-fat and low-salt, mostly for carry-out. The concept, though, was well ahead of its time and after much effort and a loss of $500,000, it closed. Then it was onward to new pursuits for the Bodines in the gentle southerly isles.

Meanwhile, the company marched onward as before.

V

Business, Family Style During the 1990s

OVER THE YEARS, THE COMPANY CONTINUED growingand became the largest manufacturer of fluorescent emergency ballasts in the country. By 1991, it was chalking up average sales of $10 million a year and turning out some 1,200 ballasts per day.

That same year, a local avionics company was having trouble getting off the ground until the Bodine Co., proposed teaming up. Harbin Electronics Co. was then a seven year-old Memphis-based, home-grown company. It needed to jump-start its line of products for the aircraft industry. By then, the Bodine Co. had earned a reputation for emergency lighting equipment, as well as for circuit boards and related equipment. Because Bodine's own-ers felt too vulnerable to the ups and downs of the construction industry, they wanted to diversify. Harbin caught their eye.

Harbin Electronics and Bodine Co. entered into about six months of discussions that resulted in a partnership in which Bo-dine purchased a 50 percent interest in Harbin. Using electronic and computer technology, Harbin Electronics had developed devices capable of testing avionics in a fraction of the time taken by traditional means. The company planned to make new similar products with the help of Bodine Co. However, that arrange-ment did not last the test of time and eventually was dissolved.

As the Bodine Co. continued to grow, it also continued to in-vest in the area's cultural arts, part of its continued emphasis on

The original lobby of the plant, showing the home-style feel that this building had until the fire.

investing in the community. In 1993, the company bought a 19th century French painting from a private collection in London and gave it to Memphis' Dixon Gallery and Gardens. The painting by Edmond Georges Grandjean was displayed at the 1882 Paris Salon. It depicts a coach drawn by two horses turning into an open space before brick buildings. Mounted on one of the horses is a young groom. Then-Dixon director John Buchanan said that the Bodine donation marked the first time that a company had bought a painting and given it to the museum's permanent collection, marking a kind of turning point for Dixon's form of acquisitions.

The very next year, the Society of Entrepreneurs inducted Dick and Jinnie Bodine into its Hall of Fame because of their accomplishments and generous contributions to Memphis' civic interests. It enshrined their thoughts on entrepreneurship with Dick's wording: "The willingness to believe in one's self and take a chance to create something new is one of the things that always made this country special and contributed to its growth. I believe this is just as important now as it has been in the past."

Longtime friend and venture capitalist Herbert Rhea reminisced that he had more than an inkling that the Bodines would be successful in their ventures even when they were still working from their Dogwood residence. "I knew them when they started off and liked them both," Herbert said. "They had just lost their son and I was so impressed with both of them and their dedication to what they were trying to accomplish. They worked as a team and you knew they would make it." They certainly did in many definitions of the term.

For some years, Herbert lost contact with the Bodines and their company until years later when he became acquainted with Al Lyons and David Crippen at Dixon Gallery and Gardens, where they were all involved as benefactors.

"I noticed the company was supporting things all over the city and I am a big believer in that," Herbert said

Beth Hoople had her own recollections of the early days when women were moving into their own in the business world. "Even with networking and joining professional organizations, mentoring was difficult to find sometimes," she said. "Early on, I decided to ask Jinnie about handshaking. When meeting men in the business world, some seemed uncomfortable — or unaware — that it was quite permissible for a woman to shake hands upon introduction. I asked Jinnie how to tell when the occasion demanded a handshake."

"Always," she replied. If the man did not offer a handshake during the introduction, she said, then it was up to the woman to initiate it.

"For years after that," Beth recalled, "whenever I saw a man hesitate before shaking hands, I silently thanked Jinnie for being able to confidently initiate what is now rather ordinary business etiquette today."

Along with those who were there near the beginning, like Beth, new and vital employees would continue to join the Bodine Co.

John Levesque, who began working with Bodine in 1988, really started to make his mark in the 1990s and that has continued through to the present. John, who during recent years worked as national sales manager at the Bodine Co., started out as a junior product engineer and progressed to product engineering supervisor of the Western area, and then to Eastern sales manager, *TranBAL*® sales manager, and ultimately to the national sales manager spot. He has followed the company tradition of innovation of products and has transferred that know how into innovation with sales strategies. Most recently, John has become president of the company.

"Over the years, we picked up new and substantial business in Canada, assisting in creating products for those markets," John said. "It grew to parallel our type of industry in the U.S. with fluorescent ballasts, however with different voltages and distinct life safety codes." He had his sales people travel throughout the provinces of Canada, learning the markets and training reps and customers on the product lines.

"Introducing new products was always kind of a challenge," John said. "It is missionary work at first in finding a new market." In a word, much introducing, training and educating went into every successful or even hopeful sale. "The same thing happened in Mexico in terms of the growth of the market and hiring reps and visiting with OEM manufacturers," John said. "In Mexico, though, we found the added challenge of the language barrier, so we had to work with the right people to have the understanding on both sides of exactly what we sought to achieve."

John vividly recalled that there was a small amount of Bodine Co. product in the World Trade Center during the first bombing back in 1991. When that happened in the tunnel under the build-

Lunch and break room with the ever-present
ping-pong tables in the foreground.

ing, it took out the power generation and the water supply, so the terrorist act basically shut down the systems. Therefore, there was no emergency lighting throughout the towers in the aftermath.

"Almost immediately after understanding the problem there, they installed thousands of Bodine battery packs throughout the stairwells in those towers," John said. "Our belief and understanding was that on Sept. 11, Bodine products were in place to provide emergency lighting and they did their jobs. Our products are designed for life-safety. Knowing they are in positions to do their jobs for bad times for people, it makes us as a company even prouder of our work."

In the Detroit and New York City markets, life safety codes have become more stringent over time and that influences yet other cities. The inspectors or authorities having jurisdiction now have a much stronger understanding of Bodine's products and have encouraged even greater coverage of safety lighting for emergency eventualities with each passing year. One of the latest emphases has been on outdoor egress lighting so the goal is not only to get people out of the building, but safely away from it.

Dan Elkins, *Tran*-BAL® product manager, started with the company in the mid- 1990s. "I've been able to enjoy the legacy the Bodines left," he said. "From the first time I interviewed for the *Tran*-BAL® engineering position, it was apparent this was a different type of company. As I took a tour of the plant, people were setting up for the annual Thanksgiving Dinner. After I was hired a couple months later, it didn't take long to understand what a great place this was to work. There seemed to always be a family-type atmosphere. We enjoyed celebrating the holidays like Thanksgiving and Christmas with big meals and there was a costume contest each Halloween."

Another highlight of the year for Dan was the company picnic at a park. "The men-versus-women tug-of-war was always a challenge because there were so many women, the men never stood a chance," he said. "But it was always a lot of fun."

Another legacy the Bodines left the company was a continuing passion for ping pong.

"Although I missed him in his prime, I have heard Dick was quite a player," Dan said. "I did get to see him hit a few around at one of our company events one time, and I would have to agree he was an excellent player. Ping pong provided many hours of fun at lunch times and after work many days a week. We even had a couple of tournaments with many participants."

Dan also noted a lot of other little things that made this company so special such as stopping work for an extended break on a hot day to enjoy watermelon or ice cream or having drawings for free hams around the holidays. But there were some big things as well. Every year, there is Employee Appreciation Night, which is a large dinner with dancing, prizes and recognition awards for years of service.

Then there also was "bonus day." The Bodines always shared a piece of the profit with all the employees. On this day, the leaders of the company then — David Crippen, Al Lyons, Jim Cagle,

Alex Ertz and Gregg Mosley — helped in staging a cookout for the entire company and distributed bonus checks that were almost always a significant part of the employees' income. Because of everyone's hard work throughout the year, they all were part of sharing the profits.

"The Bodines blessed so many people by making them part owners of the company," Dan said. "They really believed in rewarding those who spent a large portion of their lives here. In addition to the stock ownership, they instituted a retirement plan that was second to none. Although I was not around when most of the stock was distributed, I have been blessed by the way they took care of us through the retirement plan."

During the years he has worked at Bodine, Dan has seen the business grow tremendously. "It has been great to be a part of a company that has introduced new, innovative products that lead the way in emergency lighting," he said. "It's been fun and challenging to work with the *Tran*-BAL® inverter ballasts all these years." He describes the circuits as the stepping stones into the emergency ballast market. There are still small specialty markets that need *Tran*-BAL® products, so his group has enjoyed designing and meeting customers' special requests.

"It has allowed me to develop a good knowledge of the circuits and enjoy business relationships in a unique way because I have been on both the engineering and sales sides of the *Tran*-BAL® business."

In addition to the business success, Dan notes that he's very proud to be associated with a company that is so committed to the community. "There is a great commitment to the local theater and the arts. It is always special anytime someone asks me about seeing Bodine as a primary sponsor for the Public Broadcasting System....There is just a rich heritage with the Bodine Co. and so many reasons to feel proud of where I work."

Additionally, Dan's career at Bodine and the growth of his family are intertwined. He and his wife had their first child about a month after he started working there. They then had two more children within three years, so their family has grown up with Bodine. "It's all my children know and I'm proud of that. Bodine has always been very family friendly. Management wants you to enjoy time with your family. There has always been a time for hard work, but they made certain there was also a time to play and be with your family."

In retirement, Dick and Jinnie did not stay idle as some do. They continued their philanthropic spirit once they moved to the Virgin Islands. A major interest for Jinnie was the St. George Village Botanical Garden. A master plan that called for a new visitor center and an enlarged gift shop was five years in the making. Dick and Jinnie agreed to pay for the new building, which then was estimated to cost about $300,000. It was announced in the gardens newsletter and the board decided to name it the Virginia and Richard Bodine Pavilion and Courtyard. However, as happens sometimes with nonprofit organizations, there was a change of the board leadership. The new board decided the original plan was not appropriate and discarded it. With a different architect, a new building, courtyard and other features were developed.

Yet Jinnie would never see its completion. After undergoing chemotherapy treatments for breast cancer since the late 1990s, Jinnie became ill and died of heart failure on Sept. 4, 1999, at the age of 76. A strong and independent businesswoman, Jinnie had made a name for herself in Memphis at a time when not many women were entrepreneurs. Her no-nonsense style at the company and her generous spirit made her one of Memphis' most accomplished businesswomen. The school and company had lost a benefactor and friend and Dick had lost a dear lifelong partner.

Turn of the New Century and Beyond: Passing it Onward

T HE BODINE COMPANY NO LONGER IS AN operation nestled among the trees of rural Collierville. It is a multi-building complex employing almost 200 people and is now part of a multinational company. Yet the old-style charm remains through the lives of its employees, many of whom have worked for the company 15 or 20 years.

Machines that Dick and Jinnie had never seen during their tenure are part of the vast operation's network of making and testing equipment. A special set of R&D labs show a certain high-tech sophistication, with awards and advanced degree certificates to prove the hard-earned work. There, a visitor sees ample space for

One view of part of the plant during a visit in 2006.

A scene in the research and development lab.

research and development of microprocessor controls for industrial products, a printing division and a design section for printed circuit boards.

The Bodine facility originally was designed with what one might consider a touch of home: a tiled atrium that resembled a residential patio. Even back in the early years, Jinnie thought visitors to the plant should encounter a certain style and novel finish. (Sadly, this part of the company was since lost in a fire, an event that is detailed in another chapter).

The gymnasium-sized dining room is filled with various barbecue cooking contest trophies on the serving counter. Another feature of this dining room is the presence of pool and ping pong tables.

The year 2002 saw the company's pace charge ahead to the extent that it started overtime shifts for the first time ever, Gregg Mosley said. That continued for two or three years as the business grew by leaps and bounds. It also marked the first time temps were hired for the production area because the production volume was so intense.

David, Peggy, Dick, Al at the Bodine booth,
Memphis in May International Festival.

Many other full-time employees' stories continue to add to the richness of the Bodine fabric.

Mike Singleton has been involved since 1996 in various youth programs in the Memphis area and has served as the leader of the Presbyterian Youth Connection in Memphis. That organization brings youths from the Mid-South together for fellowship and faith exploration. Mostly, he helps its members create retreats. Mike also serves as the Scout Master for Boy Scout Troop 364, so it's not uncommon for him to be camping in the wilderness. Mike's troop has been cave spelunking, backpacking, scuba diving and canoeing. In addition, he has served on the planning committee for the Pinecrest Retreat & Conference Center which runs a series of summer camps. Mike considers himself fortunate to work at Bodine because it is a company that allows his personality to emerge from time to time.

*Hognado DeSoto Memphis In May booth. Note
the attention to architectural detail.*

Each year, The Bodine Company, its employees and more than 250 invited guests get together for Memphis In May World Championship Barbecue Cooking Contest. Spain was the honorary country in 2007, for instance, and Bodine certainly did its share to make Memphis' Spanish heritage known.

The business in 2008 creatively mixed historic fact and tongue-in-cheek fiction to recreate, in true Memphis in May style, the expedition of Spanish explorer Hernando DeSoto through the southeastern U.S. in the 1500s. DeSoto may have been in search of gold and a new route to China, but Bodine's fictional "Hognando de Soto" was happy to find pork and a beautiful riverfront on which to eat it. Bodine celebrated Hognando's 1541 discovery of the Mississippi River and the first barbecue in the New World by throwing its own four-day party. Bodine's Hognando de Soto booth won the festival's Best Booth Competition and was featured in a Food Network special on the BBQ festival. Its Hognando t-shirt design placed second in the Team

Alex, Dick, David and Al during an award banquet.

Shirt Competition. And out of the 110 BBQ teams competing in the prestigious rib category, Bodine's ribs ranked 33. Also, Bodine's Mustard Sauce placed 12th and its beans placed 20th that year. The company also has ongoing competitions among the employees for best recipes presented, as well as other competitions during the year.

Other employees live out their pastimes in different ways. Research & Development Manager David Crenshaw, an avid runner and martial arts enthusiast, came to the R&D department in 1991. He has four patents granted for the RCT and a patent for the ARC Keeper, in addition to two more patents pending. He became interested in electronics first through the technology of TVs and at age 9, he started taking parts from old radios to build audio hi-fi amplifiers. He worked for Peavey Electronics in the 1970s after graduating from junior college. David later studied audiometry, acoustics, physics and mathematics. He also had pursued broadcast engineering. Since then, David attained a bachelor of science degree and master of science in electrical engineering and a professional certification in power electronics. He serves as head of engineering and research and development at Bodine.

"I never actually worked for Dick and Jinnie, but I've learned from others who did," David said. "They left a legacy; their influence on others is reflected in their leadership style as well as their values and principles. (It is evident that) they really cared about the people who worked here and treated them like family.

"Later, I learned of their enormous philanthropy," David said. "After they retired, Dick and Jinnie would come visit us a couple of times a year. They walked around and made conversation with everyone. Once they met you, you were no longer a stranger. During my conversations with Dick, I've learned a lot from him. I can see that their style of leadership had the characteristics of true entrepreneurs: competency, innovation, ability to face challenges and to spot opportunity, the desire to create and deliver true value, and generosity to employees.

"I can also see that they developed people," he continued. "They were trustful of others and helped people actualize their potential. One other characteristic that struck me is that they were principled leaders. I remember we once learned that one of our competitors had initiated a rather unscrupulous act. Even though Dick was retired, his comment to us was, 'Never mind how they choose to act; we should never stoop to their level; rather, we should continue moving forward doing the right thing. The truth will find them out in due time.' Sure enough, the truth did find the company out eventually without Bodine Co.'s intervention, David said, without further elaboration.

Bodine has more recent milestones that stand out in its history. Not long ago, the Bodine Co. was involved in developing a product for the New York Transit Authority (NYTA). Its project comprised the emergency lighting framework for the New York

A transformer winding machine in a production cycle.

subway tunnels and it had to meet the requirements created by an engineering firm there for the subways exactly. The units had to withstand blast and vibration tests, corrosion, moisture and a four-hour run time, John Levesque said.

"We are supplying 3,200 inverters for the transit authority to provide four hours of emergency lighting for these subway tunnels, " Alex Ertz noted. "This is funded by the Department of Homeland Security and the product must even be able to survive bomb blasts and other heavy environmental requirements, in addition."

For this ambitious project, the company was challenged by the nuances of product definition, engineering challenges, costs, and the feasibility of this new entrepreneurial opportunity. The design specifications kept changing. At one point, things simply appeared discouraging as the specifications were modified.

Then, Dick showed up one day and asked how the project was coming along. "After I explained where we were, Dick offered some very encouraging guidance, pointing out that innovation takes risks and perseverance. Besides, the further we go with this, the more difficult it will be for competitors to copy," Alex recalled Dick saying. We moved forward, facing one challenge after another to complete the project."

Its product diversification now is almost dizzying. The Bodine Co. has emergency lighting solutions and products for many different applications, such as a series for damp locations and vapor-tight applications and another series for generator-supplied fluorescent lighting. There are also ballasts for compact fixtures, low-profile fixtures and hazardous locations.

In essence, products are available for indoor/dry, damp and hazardous location fixtures and may be modified to accommodate voltages, line frequencies and longer run times. Other Bodine Co. products include linear fluorescent lamps that serve as a mainstay in commercial, industrial and institutional lighting. There also are compact fluorescent emergency ballasts and low-profile fluorescent emergency ballasts which are ideal for pendant, cove, recessed, low-profile and other space-limited lighting applications.

There even are specially designed lighting fixtures for hospitals and emergency rooms. For operating rooms, for instance, the high-illumination output is geared for a sufficient enough run time to transition surgeons and their patients between a power failure and a startup of a generator for backup lighting, John Levesque explained.

To keep it in perspective, though, the company was always an innovator at the core and its central products serve as the tree trunk for the various limbs of offerings sprouting almost by the month.

"To me, our first self-testing product was a huge step with having a microprocessor in an emergency ballast," production manager Gregg Mosley said. "Then, we had the remote control self-test units and that was really something."

Today, emergency lighting has become a vital part of every facility's safety system. National, state and local building codes, including National Electrical Code®, the Life Safety Code® and OSHA require reliable and sufficient emergency illumination for all commercial, industrial and institutional buildings. In the event of emergencies, this lighting guides occupants to exits, helps prevent injury en route and plays a key role in the swift and successful passage of occupants to safety.

Bodine's fluorescent emergency ballasts, often referred to as fluorescent battery packs, provide instant backup lighting when normal power fails. Each emergency ballast now contains a high-temperature nickel-cadmium battery, charger and electronic circuitry in one compact case.

Lately, the company also has been bringing back national-level and singular honors from an annual event known as the Light-fair International exhibition. It is the premier annual lighting trade show in North America and features architectural and commercial lighting products. "It's a very a big show with large stages and screen projection units," Dick said. "They award prizes and recognition in various categories. One of them would be, for instance, for the design of a new type of light bulb." Bodine had won again in 2007, he said, smiling broadly.

Bodine is still inventing, solving problems and creating new products. Here is a rundown of its primary product groupings.

Bodine's REDiTEST self-diagnostic fluorescent ballasts automatically test emergency lighting at intervals according to code. This means building maintenance personnel aren't required to manually test emergency lighting each month, saving building owners and operators time and money.

The FEBnet system automates and integrates all emergency lighting systems within a building with controls from a centralized PC. It automatically tests and monitors each emergency ballast in the network and alerts the system manager if a problem occurs.

The ARC Keeper® HID Backup Ballast helps eliminate downtime in metal halide lighting systems by supporting the lamp arc for up to two minutes during a power disturbance. This product anticipates that power is beginning to fail in a facility. At the very instant that kind of situation occurs, every other high intensity discharge light goes off and this specialty type of light comes on fully. The challenge of manufacturing such a device was to make something that anticipates power failures and automatically activates when the power is about to fail, if even for an instant. In essence, this is a smart circuit that tracks line voltage and any interruptions.

ARC Keeper's entire line offers a breakthrough technology for metal halide lighting systems. Such lamps function as the primary lighting source in facilities such as grocery stores, warehouses and gymnasiums. These are facilities particularly sensitive to power fluctuations. Even more than their use in sports facilities and gyms though, these ARC Keepers are used for parking garage areas that have an even greater need for life safety coverage.

LEDs (light emitting diodes) are transforming the lighting industry, showing up in everything from traffic lights to flashlights. The Bodine Co. offers power supplies for a variety of LED lighting applications such as step lights and down lights. Philips, which acquired the company in 2008, has won international awards now for designs of LEDs. At the end of a recent ceremony, the master award for the product of the year went to the ARC Keeper. "All the Philips people were really cheering for that award-naming," Dick said.

Even the *Tran*-BAL® , the cornerstone of the company, has been modified and improved. The devices now can convert AC or DC power into high-frequency AC power to start and operate most lamp types, including fluorescent, low-pressure sodium,

Dick and longtime employee, Angie in the Graphic Arts deparment.

germicidal and ultraviolet lamps. No other ballast or starter is required. They continue to provide vehicle lighting in ambulances, buses, commercial vans and subways and are a flicker-free light source for photoelectric applications, inspection systems, scanning equipment and reprographic equipment.

FEBnet and the LED emergency driver were first-place winners at Lightfair International in 2004. FEBnet also received one of Lightfair's special recognition prizes, the Technical Innovation Awards. This is presented to the Lightfair New Product Showcase entry that "represents the best leap forward in lighting technology excellence."

"The FEBnet was the apple of everyone's eye here at Bodine," said Shane DeLima, who started working on this project as an intern in 2001. "Being a newby to the real world, it seemed like a great challenge."

Tom Mascari, an R&D engineer at that time, and Shane worked on the project for about two years. They ventured into areas such as surface-mount technology and PC software development with FEBnet and other devices' development.

"Though overwhelming, we always had the support of the management at every step of this project," Shane said. "Yes, at times, we were frustrated trying to get electronics to work the way we wanted to, but their encouragement helped us to move forward. In 2004, we introduced the product at Lightfair and it was a big hit, winning two awards (the best in category in systems and also the Technical Innovation Award). Everyone was very pleased with the outcome of all our hard work. It is moments like these that make working as an R&D engineer very rewarding." Now, Tom is working as a senior manufacturing engineer at the Bodine Co. while Shane is an R&D engineer.

Dominating the fluorescent emergency lighting market with more than a 50 percent market share, Bodine's products are sold internationally and distributed through a network of manufacturers' representatives and commercial lighting fixture manufacturers. A line of the fluorescent emergency lighting ballasts are also private-labeled for numerous other emergency lighting companies.

Bodine is a member of the Illuminating Engineering Society of North America (IESNA) and the National Electrical Manufacturers Association (NEMA).

Bodine Co. equipment is in some unconventional and unusual types of locations, too. These include oil refineries, paint booths and textile mills associated with potential fire and explosion hazards, including combustible gases, liquids, dust and fibers. Bodine emergency ballasts for hazardous location fixtures contain fully sealed relays to eliminate the arcs and sparks of ignition sources.

In terms of extended temperatures, Bodine's Cold-Pak® Fluorescent Emergency Ballasts provide lighting in extreme environments.

Al, Dick, and Alex. At this time in 2006, Al was president, Dick was retired and Alex was head of research and development.

The Bodine Co. not only has a reputation for longevity of its products, but also longevity of service among its employee ranks. Length of service among employees is almost legendary and considered part of the environment. Mary Wylie, a production line operator who retired in June 2007, is indicative of the long-working employees who received their due rewards upon retirement from the company. She started working for Bodine in 1978 as an assembler in the transformer department and on the lines.

"Someone told me they were hiring and I went to the employment service, then visited with Jim Cagle and he hired me on the spot," she said. One of her specialties was winding transformers.

"Dick and Jinnie were genuine and when they told you anything, they stood behind it," Mary said. "They made working fun. When we got through with our work, we could visit with each other. They were not always watching the clock as long as you did your work. When they told us they were going to give a raise, they always stood behind it. The same with vacation time."

Retirement for Mary has been just as good. "The stock made my retirement," she said. "It was all put there by the Bodines. I am thankful and grateful for that."

A relatively newer hire, Sean Cash, started with Bodine in the fall of 2001 after a corporate and government career fair sponsored by the University of Memphis. It led to his first full-time job after graduation as a product engineer. At the career fair, Sean met Tom Stoll, his future boss and a fellow U of M alum. Before attending the fair, Sean had sent resumes to every engineering firm in Memphis.

"Bodine participates in local university career fairs and uses them as an important resource to select the best candidates for engineering and other departments," Tom said at the time. "Career fairs are a great way to market yourself to prospective employers and get feedback on what types of jobs are currently available." Tom is product engineering manager now at the Bodine Co. He's an officer in the local chapter of the Illuminating Engineering Society of North America, chair of the NEMA Emergency Lighting Section, a licensed professional engineer, and the company's liaison with Underwriters Laboratories (UL) and the Canadian Standards Association (CSA).

Sean was able to intern with Bodine for three months before his graduation in 2001. Upon graduation, he assumed a full-time position as a product engineer. "Before graduation, I did essentially the same job functions I do now," he said then. "Of course I was still learning the ropes, but my boss was good at assigning me tasks that I would be doing once working for Bodine."

Tom praised Sean's performance as a part-time and full-time employee.

"He (Sean) has turned out to be even more of an asset to our company (as an R&D engineer) than we originally thought when we hired him back in 2001," Tom said. "As a part-time employee, he took on many engineering projects and he's become a vital member of Bodine's team."

These and other illustrations demonstrate that a company's success is intertwined directly with Bodine and its people. "What has made the company special internally is the prevailing spirit of everyone being a contributor," Alex Ertz said. "We're not just a place to come work. All along, we knew we were doing something new and exciting. We are clever and customer-focused."

Externally, what makes Bodine special, Alex said, is its focus. "In the day, there were all of these lighting companies, mostly EXIT sign manufacturers, who wanted to do backup lighting," Alex recalled. "They were not that good at what they did, while we excelled because that is all we did. As David said, 'We have the intimate knowledge of the marketplace and understand the dynamics involved in the buying decision-making.' We have lived this world since the 1970s and know it better than anyone else."

Alex described the Bodines themselves as empowering entre-preneurs who believed in a young, intact management team, al-though they were just in their 30s when they were launching the company and making its mark in the industry.

"They would want you to come to them with alternatives and solutions and Dick and Jinnie did not see themselves as com-mand-and-control," Alex said. That philosophy built a certain entrepreneurial spirit in the management cadre they left behind to run the company in their stead.

"Working for a company like Bodine has been a wonderful and unique experience and I'm thankful I was given the oppor-tunity to 'grow up' in such a place," said Brad Van Frank, pro-motions manager at Bodine. "I'm proud to have been associated with a company that recognized the value and importance of the employees that contributed to its success." He affirmed how Dick and Jinnie's leadership, work ethic and philosophy influenced the management of the company.

"Everything we do, we do for the company and not to make our own lights shine," Gregg Mosley said, summing up the enterprise.

An unwelcome episode in the chronicles of the company arrived in the middle of 2008. On a May morning, the administrative portion of the business endured a very damaging after-hours fire. This intense fire affected several offices at the company, however, no employees were on site at the time it erupted. When the Collierville and area fire department units arrived, they witnessed heavy flames and smoke erupting from the entry building's administrative offices at about 10:30 p.m. on May 21st. The fire was under control by 2 the next morning.

The fire was mostly contained within one building, which housed the company's telephone systems, information technology, purchasing, accounting, bookkeeping, a mail room, and other administrative offices, along with computers and battery storage. Nearby assembly and production buildings sustained heavy smoke damage, officials said.

Collierville sent five fire trucks from all of its stations to the scene while the Germantown and Shelby County fire departments each sent one to assist. Twenty off-duty firefighters also were called, using a list an administrative secretary keeps at home. The fire damaged all six buildings in the complex on Mount Pleasant Road at South Street.

"Even the farthest building was coated inside with soot," Dick said. There also was extensive water damage. Decades old, the burning building had a metal roof and sides plus three ceilings firefighters discovered one by one by ripping them down.

Initial fire investigations thought the source of the fire could have originated from the battery charging system area. Bodine employees, after being allowed on the site, carried out computers and other undamaged equipment.

"There was such extensive smoke damage involving dramatic cleanups," Dick said after getting a phone briefing from current management. "Every page of every book that the company needs to retain had to be cleaned page by page."

"Basically, we had an oven," said Collierville Fire Chief Jerry Crawford. Firefighters used a record 120 air bottles while battling the blaze. In addition, police controlled traffic and onlookers. Public service employees boosted the water pressure.

The Collierville Chamber of Commerce offered services to the Bodine Co., including the uses of its office space at its center. The Bodine Co. has been a loyal Chamber member and community supporter for 24 years. "The Chamber was proud to be able to help The Bodine Company in their time of need," said Fran Persechini, chamber president. Due to the fire, smoke and water damage to their facility, they were in immediate need of office space and communication resources (phone, internet, copy and fax capabilities) in order to maintain limited services. We are very fortunate to have a facility that could accommodate approximately 35 employees for two weeks."

In addition to that, the Chamber was able to do some of the legwork through its network of resources, and researched available warehouse space, tenting, and temporary modular buildings. It also shared its very headquarters with Bodine Co. staff for a time on Halle Park Drive after the fire.

"The Bodine Company has a strong history of giving back to our chamber and community," Fran added. "We had many champions who significantly contributed to the success of our economic development initiative." In fact, the Bodine Co. had helped the chamber build its building and conduct an economic development program. "The Bodine Company can be counted among those champions, Fran continued. "It is an honor and privilege to have the opportunity to assist the Bodine Company and its employees in any way possible."

Bodine management organized restoration teams soon after the fire. The large tents were set up for the extensive cleaning and a storage bin was ordered onsite. The vault where records were kept was sound and thus its contents were safe and undamaged. Also, the plant daily backed up its data and once a week, a copy also was sent offsite.

By the first week of June, the company was able to get the wire machines running. However, soot and water started its slow but sure damage, oxidizing metals that had not been fully cleaned. While the business was able to start limited production in stages during the first week of June, about two months passed after the fire before the assembly line would be fully running again.

That eventuality came, in part, sooner than expected — in the first week of July. That date marked the first time all permanent assembly workers were back on the job after the fire. Knowing the spirit of the company, it will not only recover, it will also continue to flourish.

VII

The Purchase by Philips and Going Global

I N 2006, NETHERLANDS-BASED ROYAL PHILIPS Electronics — one of the world's largest makers of electronics and lighting products — acquired the company for an undisclosed amount. Philips has 162,000 employees in 60 countries and annual revenues of more than $35 billion; Bodine had annual revenues averaging $30 million.

Both the Bodine Co. and Philips spoke confidently that the union would help advance the lighting industry, add value for customers and provide users with new opportunities for technical innovations, sales growth and cost reductions. At the time of the purchase, Phillips announced its intentions to retain the name and operations much as they had been, capitalizing on a good thing. As a result of the sale, Bodine Co. now has more international export markets. In turn, Philips was attracted by Bodine's skilled work force and management leadership.

"The purchase did come as a surprise to me and viewing it now, it was a good decision and they did pick a good company to sell to," Dick Bodine said.

Dick recalls a now-humorous and frantic search for requested paperwork at the cusp of the transaction. "They needed the private stock certificates," he said. Dick didn't know where Jinnie had placed them, even though he knew she would be meticulous about such a thing. "They said, 'We've got to have them or we'll have to post a bond," he recalled. Then Dick brainstormed and looked in the only place not yet investigated – a closet at the Memphis condominium. Therein, he jimmied open a box in a second drawer of a file cabinet and located the much-sought papers.

"The stock certificates represented the 50 percent share of the company owned by me and the other half owned by Jinnie," Dick said. "If we could not find them, we would be unable to prove that the ones selling the company really owned it. We should have given them to the company (years earlier) after they finished paying off the loan. After that period of time since Jinnie's death, it had not occurred to anyone."

Negotiations with Philips had been in the works less than a year before the purchase and the transaction brought together two companies with leading market share in their respective areas: Bodine in emergency lighting and Philips in a bevy of health care and consumer-related products such as medical diagnostic imaging and patient monitoring, color television sets and electric shavers.

"This acquisition positions Philips very favorably in the niche emergency ballast market and enables us to broaden our product portfolio and enter strategic new market segments," said Brian Dundon, president and CEO of Philips Lighting Electronics North America. Specifically, the company has seen increased importance placed on the emergency lighting segment since 9/11 and saw an opportunity with a key product.

"The acquisition of Bodine is intended to expand Philips Lighting Electronics' offering into an adjacent product line, enable Philips to expand into new markets, and enhance Philips' value proposition within the lighting industry," said David Levinson, vice president of marketing and product management for Philips Lighting Electronics North America.

Al, one of the Philips Electronics' executives, and Dick pose during the employee appreciation night function.

Bodine and Philips Lighting have complementary product offerings and shared some of the same customers. By combining the two they can "optimize those synergies" and grow Bodine's business. Soon after the acquisition, then Bodine president Al Lyons remarked, "As we become integrated, both will be committed to leveraging both strengths and opportunities to enhance and optimize the business."

Although Bodine has continued to grow and gain market share, it became obvious that being part of a larger company could allow the company to maximize its potential more easily, Al said at the time. Like many companies, Bodine had received many acquisition offers over the years, but Philips was finally the one that made sense and seemed to provide desired benefits, he added.

In addition to Philips giving Bodine the ability to go global, according to Alex Ertz, the acquisition helps in additional areas such as an advanced contract review system before agreements are presented for signature and also assists in the process of gaining patents on select new products. Moreover, the combined enterprise places representatives in corners of the world Bodine never had before. "We've greatly increased our sales to Mexico, Latin America and the Middle East as a result. Export sales increased by some 400 percent in 2007 over the prior year," Alex said.

As for Bodine's attractiveness to Philips' management, Alex said, "We were the biggest, most established leader in emergency ballast lighting in the U.S. and customers were fully satisfied with our products, prices and promotions. This effectively let Philips enter this market."

Alex said that some advantages of the merger were seen within the first few months with increased production capacity being a major benefit. "We were in a bottleneck with production," he added. "Sales had increased and we were stretched with our facility and employees. Going to two shifts would not be easy." Philips is having some 40 percent of Bodine's products built in Tijuana, but only the high volume, more basic units. Meanwhile, the newer and also more complex products still are being assembled in Collierville.

Not only that, but employees also benefited directly in a financial way. About 100 employees were ESOP shareholders at the time of the sale to Philips. They saw their share prices rise substantially over the original price and just about double right at the point of acquisition from the amount paid by Philips, Alex added.

In the final analysis, the hard-won market recognition that the Bodine Co. had worked to build up over the decades paid off. "Our brand identity is so important to Philips that it wants us to continue it," said Brad Van Frank.

THE BODINE STORY

VIII

Giving Back to the Community

Editor's Note: Until this chapter, the Bodine story has been told in chronological fashion for logical continuity reasons, as the company grew. From this point onward, the book will proceed with thematic chapters, which proves most logical since certain umbrella themes are best discussed with in that format and cover different areas in their treatments.

FOR THE BODINES, COMMUNITY REINVESTMENT was never just a corporate duty or obligation. It was a way of life and almost naturally transferred to the company mindset over time. The company has become a generous contributor to many social, civic and educational programs in the Memphis area.

"It's a company tradition and something we want to do," said Al Lyons, the company's immediate past president. Al, who retired in 2008, exemplifies the commitment to community service that has been a hallmark of the Bodine Co. He served as the interim director of Memphis Brooks Museum of Art until a permanent director was hired. In 2009, he became the board president of the Memphis in May International Festival, Inc. He also continues to serve in a consultancy role for the Bodine Co.

That tradition of service started in the early days with Dick and Jinnie. They respected the time-honored practice of tithing the first fruits of their labor on a personal basis; and soon applied what they had learned about church-giving and transformed that philosophy into a rare corporate tradition. Namely, the company gave a percentage of its gross sales revenues to philanthropies.

Myung & Mathew (4) Ku, Mr. & Mrs. Bodine,
Steve Pike at the Pink Palace.

Jinnie explains the philosophy in her 1995 letter — "Ten percent came out at the beginning. It worked so well that I carried the idea over to the company – 10 percent to savings before paying vendors, employees, taxes, etc. It was used for employee benefits – annual bonuses, a profit-sharing plan (for retirement), an employee stock ownership plan and for contributions."

Dick hadn't always thought that way, although he grew up in the church. He admits that for many years, he was stingy and didn't want to give. "At that time, I was so tight that I was unable to give anything without it hurting," Dick said. Faith changed that mindset over time, though, and God gave him the ability to share what God had given him.

"Fortunately, God did take a hand in it and that changed me. It started with the decision to tithe," Dick said. "That was decided because we had no income at the time we started the school and company and 10 percent of nothing was an amount I could handle. Once the change started, it made me realize it was easy and rewarding to share what I had." There even was enough left over to give to the community.

"Our continued support is strong in education, sports, children's programs, the arts, medical research and healthcare for the poor," David Crippen said.

The Bodines also have contributed personally to the building campaign of the Pink Palace Museum and are life-long members of the Dixon Gallery and Gardens. Dick and Jinnie Bodine's entrepreneurial spirit, leadership and charitable contributions have made a positive and lasting impact on many lives in the Memphis metropolitan area.

Their concern for others extended not only to the community, but also to their employees. Whenever someone at the Bodine Co. knew of a family in need, Dick and Jinnie sponsored an outreach program to help with food, clothing or Christmas gifts.

The company also looks after the Bodine School. Every year, Bodine employees take the big grill they use for Memphis in May over to the school grounds and provide an end-of-the-school-year picnic for the parents and students.

The benefits of this charitable giving often have gone far beyond simply rescuing people in need. The employees also have found this a compelling reason to be proud of being part of The Bodine Company. Beth Hoople, who left the company when her former husband transferred out of town, said, "I can't count the number of times when I told someone I worked for Bodine, that they replied that their son, cousin or neighbor had been helped tremendously by attending The Bodine School. And, when we actually met the people who were being helped, the faces of those receiving food and clothing is so unforgettable. The happiness of the kids getting Christmas presents when their parents had not been able to give them a Christmas remains indelibly in my memories.

"You can't put a price on that kind of job satisfaction," Beth said. "It goes far beyond the material benefits of stock ownership, a bonus check or a company picnic. And, sadly, the rarity of such corporate generosity adds to the feeling of pride."

A community involvement committee at the Bodine Co. each year revisited giving objectives for the business. Representatives from all the departments were involved. The company has had Purchasing, Accounting, Production, Sales, Engineering and Printing departments for most of the course of its history and everyone seemed to want to serve on the committee. Jinnie would give them the budget and then they would investigate who needed money.

Once, the owner of another local company heard about the program and asked about setting up a similar one for his business. "We'd been getting some publicity about it and he came over and asked how it worked," Dick said. "We told him. He said, 'Where do they get the money?' We replied, 'You give them the money,' and that killed it right there with him."

The Bodine Co. for instance, discussed and voted to contribute to two projects in 1981. One was the then very needy Hollywood Childcare Center. The center cared for children from 15 months old to 5 years old, most of whom were referred by the Tennessee Department of Human Services. It occupied space in a former Memphis City Schools building and was never properly funded.

"Jinnie had met the guy running it," Dick said. "It was operating on a shoestring." The center kept children all day, taught them in classes and fed them lunch. It lacked in bookkeeping and

The Pink Palace Museum.

got into trouble with the state for that reason. Jinnie would go work with Hollywood Childcare on their books and even bought them a computer for their staff to use. "We went to Nashville with them one time to help them through their questionnaires," Dick said. Some funds just disappeared – not out of malfeasance, but because they did not know how to conduct accounting properly, he said.

The company would gather children's names and ages and buy them gifts, wrapping them for each child. A few days before Christmas, Santa Claus would dress up and employees would run a shuttle and drive out to the day care center. That lasted maybe three years. The state ultimately shut the childcare center down because of internal mismanagement.

Long interested in the Memphis Pink Palace Museum, the Bodines made serious contributions after retirement, too. The couple had been invited to the Pink Palace one night at a small group meeting where museum officials asked for pledges to

Dick with Bodine Students.

expand the Pink Palace and to help build the IMAX Theater. The presenters handed out envelopes and many of those present would respond. "We opened ours and they wanted $5,000, so that started our relationship with the Pink Palace," Dick said. A major upstairs wing there is named after them.

Doug Noble, who was director of the Memphis museum system at the time, also got the couple involved in the expansion and IMAX, which grew into a sizeable endeavor. Dick and Jinnie were invited to introduce Tony Yanaro, one of the stars of the IMAX theatre film, "To the Limit," for its grand opening. Dick and Jinnie were doing Tony's introduction on the stage with a large backdrop. They acted like the famous mountain climber had not arrived. About that time, Tony rappelled from the ceiling on a rope.

Doug did not know Dick and Jinnie until their involvement with the museum system. "As director, I wanted to know, 'Who were these people sending us an unsolicited check?'" Thanks to

Bob Sharpe Sr., Doug soon found out and a relationship quickly formed.

Neither of the Bodines had ever been to Graceland, so once Doug and his wife, Taffy, arranged for a VIP tour for them. The trip must have been a resounding success because Dick enjoys telling the story and proudly displays their VIP Graceland tickets.

The Graceland tour was going to be tough to top. Yet several years later, when Dick had married Peggy Jemison, Doug discovered that they hadn't been to the gambling Mecca of Tunica. He and Taffy arranged a limousine to drive them down and bring them back after a big night on the town. The stretch limo arrived late, Doug recalled, and that may have been an omen of what was to come.

"We were dropped at our first casino and had dinner," he said. "From that point on, the transportation went downhill. From limo to shuttle bus, to van, we made our way back to Memphis in less-than-grand style." Evidently, the casinos discovered they weren't such big-time high rollers and the mode of transportation thus descended as time passed on.

When Doug speaks of the Bodines, he describes their "overwhelming" generosity and says they taught him much about philanthropy and a giving spirit. "In a time when our nation is obsessed with talk about heroes, I can honestly say that both Taffy and I think of you as a good man of heroic proportions in your thoughts, words and deeds," he noted in a written and spoken tribute during Dick's 80th birthday celebration. The Nobles' relationship with the Bodines didn't end with the Nobles' own move from Memphis however, and they have maintained a good friendship. Doug now heads exhibits and public programs at the Florida Museum of Natural History in Gainesville. The Nobles and Dick and Peggy got together, for instance, when Peggy was visiting Albany, Ga., to take a look at one of the first Holiday Inns her husband, Frank, had invested in many years ago. It was a good occasion for the four of them to spend time together and have lunch.

When one of the Nobles' daughters, Jenny, was considering locations for her wedding, she decided on St. Croix; the location would never have crossed her mind if she didn't know of her parents' friends enjoying their life there to such a degree. (Doug and Taffy have another daughter, Kate). All enjoyed the family event at the Carambola resort there.

The current director of museums for Memphis, Steve Pike, is also over the Pink Place Family of Museums and shares the Nobles' admiration for the Bodines. "My deepest impression of Dick and Peggy is that both are incredibly down-to-earth people who truly want to help others," Steve said. "I have a clear memory of them at dinner at our house one evening. Dick was talking about the early days of the school, a time when he was not sure how to keep it afloat financially. They received the donation out of the blue that was much larger than they had expected and they were able to keep the school going. I remember clearly seeing the emotion on Dick's face as he spoke about it."

Steve also recalled an occasion when the museum was putting together a master plan to bring many new things to the city. "I asked Dick and Peggy for help in the early stages," he said. "This is the hardest part, the 'lift off.' They listened thoughtfully and then said, 'Yes.' A lot of people have a hard time making a decision like that, but Dick and Peggy know their minds and their hearts."

In 2007, during one of Dick and Peggy's visits to the museum, Steve showed them the exhibit that was housed in the Bodine Exhibit Hall at the time. It was an interactive exhibit on the science of music and there were a lot of children enjoying it. "You could see the delight in Dick's and Peggy's eyes as they watched the kids learning and having fun at it," he said. A 2008 exhibit in the Bodine Wing explored the treasure-hunting lore with extensive exhibits. Other themes would follow.

By 2008, the Sharpe Planetarium reopened weekdays in addition to Saturdays. Funding for the expanded hours was provided in part by Dick and Peggy as sponsors of the Bodine Series of Planetarium school programs. In addition, the Bodines have funded the new Pink Palace website, the Bodine Collecting Program in Mid-South History and the Bodine Education Forum.

The Bodine Company also has served as a sponsor of WKNO/PBS shows because of its overriding support of teaching and education. Other beneficiaries of Bodine generosity have been Brooks Memorial Art Gallery and Dixon Gallery and Gardens. The company also has supported the Germantown Performing Arts Centre (GPAC) and small community theaters in addition to MIFA's past Starry Nights project.

"The Bodines instilled in all of us the need to give something back to the community out of our success," David Crippen noted. "As the company grew and prospered, so did our donations. I think Dick and Jinnie were proud of the way we continued and increased their philanthropic endeavors."

And today, as part of Philips, that legacy continues with Bodine showing its commitment to support local arts, cultural and educational organizations.

Truly, the legacy of the contributions of both the company and the Bodine family continues because of the significant seeds they have planted over the years.

IX

The Faith Journeys

THERE'S NO UNDERESTIMATING HOW FAITH presented major spiritual challenges and changes in the Bodines' own lives over time. It affected their spiritual outlook and their business ethic.

Not only were the Bodines working to build a company, but God was at work in the lives of the Bodines to build a genuine and enduring faith. That journey gained momentum through their association with a new pastor at their church. The relationship soon grew as they worked with other families to pursue mutual objectives.

Dick and Jinnie's early spiritual growth found nurturing through Rev. Ernest Mellor's arrival at their Germantown Presbyterian Church in the 1960s after the Mellors' five years in the Brazilian mission fields. Soon, Rev. Mellor began a tradition to have family retreats at Nacome, a church campground about an hour east of Memphis. That was good timing, too, because Rick Bodine was 11 or 12 about then.

In his first year, Rev. Mellor asked a family from the national ecumenical lay ministry called Faith at Work to come to the meeting too. "I realized that we needed a closer relationship in the mid 1960s with the congregation and a friend advised me to travel to New York and get acquainted with the Faith at Work movement," Rev. Mellor recalled. "We came back and started small groups and Dick and Jinnie were active members. You got to know people well that way and it really fulfilled a need we had."

That conference marked the beginning of change in the Bodines' spiritual life.

"Ernest always thought big and we decided once to have a Mid South Faith at Work conference," his wife Lalla said. "We wrote Christian author/speaker Bruce Larson about the idea and he put it in their magazine. We started getting applications from everywhere. Because 300 showed up, we had to move the assembly to Germantown High School."

"That was the start of a change in my life," Dick said. "During the weekend, I was challenged by one of the Faith at Work people to pick a time during the day when our family was together and to have a prayer out loud together. If you were not used to doing that, it was very different. He told us that when you first announce this, your kids will think you've flipped.

"We got that reaction from my son when we announced the next week that we would have a reading from the Bible and a prayer on a daily basis. But we found out soon that we could indeed pray out loud regularly about things we found difficulty discussing." Rick was 15 at the time.

One day, the family went to a communion service on Maundy Thursday when Rick was home for Easter. Later that night as Dick and Rick were driving to go play racquetball, Rick asked his dad what communion meant to him. As Dick was trying to come up with a good, fatherly answer, Rick said, "Dad, tonight I saw the cross. Jesus was on the cross. God was above the cross and His love was flowing down through Jesus to us."

That moment would prove to help Dick through the tragedy of his son's death. "That engendered a big change in my life and Jesus became real to me," Dick said. "It helped solidify our family life and helped us get through the death of our son a couple of years later."

Ernest and Lalla Mellor.

Over time, the Bodines became more involved in Faith at Work and even led groups of people in various churches in this movement that sprang up during the 1970s as a way to build up the level of marital conversation and closeness among church goers. "Our core group would go to a church on a Friday and hold a meeting that night in which we sang choruses and got acquainted," Dick said. "On Saturdays, the meetings broke up into small groups. A lot of the time, there were more of us than members of the church attending these. We learned you cannot let that bother you. It generally petrified the preachers before-hand because they didn't know what to expect of this newfangled relational theology."

At end of every Sunday, the Faith at Work guests would "take over" the Sunday service, speaking and leading into the Peace of the Lord benedictions and responses that took place with the people in the pews next to one another. A lot of the ministry focused on the couples themselves and what they needed to say about how they felt about each other. The programs were designed to help get people in touch with their feelings. Authors and pastors Bruce Larson and Keith Miller continued to mentor the movement on a national basis.

"It gave you the opportunity to talk with people on a more intimate level and have unconditional love and broadcast that beyond our families," Dick said.

As time went on, the Mellors and Bodines accompanied each other to out-of-town churches for lay weekends as discussion team leaders and also to regional conferences. "Dick and Jinnie were really involved and supported others," Ernest Mellor said. "Some people didn't particularly like spiritual intimacy, but they did. We were drawn to them."

At about this time, a lady named Gert Bahana intersected the Bodines' lives. Rumor had it that she was a household-name philanthropist's daughter and had given away all of her money. Nonetheless, she was a rather well-known Christian speaker.

"We were all in awe of her," Dick said. "One time, we were at a Faith at Work conference in Gatlinburg, Tennessee with about 300 other people. The meeting opened with a dinner. Everyone was seated when Gert entered the room and started up the center aisle to the table where Jinnie and I were sitting. She stopped, left her escort and came straight toward our table. The closer she got to our table, the more apprehensive I became. The room got silent as she came around behind me and put her hands on my head. I was simply scared. She let the suspense increase for about 30 seconds and then in her gravelly voice said, "I guess the Lord will have to do something about that cow-lick; I can't."

The following is a quote from a former Faith at Work coordinator and Bodine friend, Jerry Hilton, describing Gert: "When she became a Christian, her life absolutely opened up. She didn't become a Christian until she was about 70 or 75 years old. When she became a Christian, one of the first things she did was give away all her money. She later said, 'That was a mistake.'

"I remember her speaking at the Lakeside Methodist Church in Oklahoma City," Jerry continued. She said, "The fact is, I could have done all kinds of good things with it, but in my haste, I got rid of it all."

The people involved in the Faith at Work movement often found a new relevance to their faith. This was the case for Dick and Jinnie, who found that the program gave them not only a real vision for their lives, but it also provided a means of the Lord to help prepare them for Rick's death. It had infused prayer into their personal lives, as well.

There were also occurrences outside church circles that some considered quite divine, Dick observed. "We then had a copy machine in the office and it needed to warm up each morning. One day, I flipped it on and without waiting, it issued forth a piece of paper that in big black letters said to "Go to church Sunday" but there was no master in there to be copied. No one knew where that piece of paper came from. We never did find out any reason or person who put it in there to do that. It was a mystery."

There was another time when Dick was working on a new product using a timer. In designing it, he found it needed a dual timer, not a single timer. But the people who made the integrated circuit did not make one. "One morning about this same time, I walked in my office, and there in the middle of my desk pad was a dual IC timer that supposedly no one made," Dick said. "I couldn't find out where that one came from, nor did I find another one. You can draw your own conclusions, but I accept these as miracles. All of this happened about the same time."

The kind of relationships cemented with Faith at Work, the Mellors, the Lord and even each other were crucial preparations for the devastating news that the Bodines would face in the death of their only child. He had learned to water ski when he was just about 5 years old. He knew water safety well, having been an Eagle Scout. Needless to say, there were many mysteries that they would find themselves grappling with – both from natural and spiritual vantage points.

Rev. Mellor, who always had a bent for counseling (he later earned his doctorate and established the Pastoral Counseling Center of Greater Memphis), was well-suited – alongside his wife, Lalla – to help counsel and encourage the Bodines during that period of their lives. The four stayed close even after Ernest went out of state and returned with his advanced degree and continued after the Bodines went with some 15 other families to help with the church planting of Faith Presbyterian Church.

"We always felt right at home to go visit their house," Ernest said. "They were ready to give a warm welcome to people, and especially to those of faith."

John and Louise Bagby are a couple who got to know the Bodines in their early years in Memphis and who mutually grew together with them in friendship over time. The Bagbys moved to Memphis in 1967 and got to know the Bodines at the same Germantown Presbyterian Church about a year later. "In 1968, we joined Germantown Presbyterian," Louise said. "In that same year, Rick died. Dick and Jinnie had wanted that child so much. They were so intent on having a family. Jinnie placed much of her affection, emotions and energy outside the company toward Rick and his needs and development. Dick wanted to assist."

Germantown Presbyterian Church had neither a finial nor a cross atop its steeple on what is now the old chapel. Dick's aunt, Elizabeth Stewart Janes, saw to it that a cross was mounted on the original church steeple and dedicated to Rick.

John Bagby and Dick became close friends through church committees on which they served. "He played good tennis and I was trying to learn and he helped me in that greatly," John said. "We won the Germantown tournament one year and that was a good deal for me. We all got together at each others' homes in Germantown. We built a tennis court. Everybody would come over and we would cook out and play tennis." Later on, Dick built a tennis court. They'd have men's doubles matches and have guests over.

There were other Dick and John adventures. "One time, a tree was about to fall on the Bodine barn and we took a chain saw over there to remove the threat in the event of a storm," John Bagby said. "Another time, I had a woodworking shop built and once the carpenters left, Dick came over one afternoon to play tennis. I told him that I had a problem and didn't know anyone who knew how to wire it. He showed me and we helped each other that way.

"We also built a deck at our house and then realized a large tree limb would fall on it if we ever had a storm," John continued. "So I got up in the tree and used some wire we had left over and we thought we had it tied off well. I cut the limb and it fell right onto the new deck anyway."

The Bagbys would sometimes visit the plant in Collierville after hours and Dick and John would have fierce ping pong matches in the break room, sometimes for two hours. "He would most often beat me."

For a short while, Dick's basement became a winemaking operation. "He called me one day and said, 'We're going to make some wine using Welch's grape juice. Bring over 15 pounds of sugar when you come.' He had a big crock down there," John recalled. "The sugar was cooked in a stove with water until it was dissolved. We added yeast and waited for a period for it to ferment. We bought a big glass jar and would drain the fermenting juice from one container to another. We'd wait a couple of weeks, then bottle it. You could drink it in the beginning, but not later on. We did several batches of the wine together.

John and Louise said Dick didn't talk about work much in his off-time and left the office at the office for the most part. "But I remember around 1980, he celebrated, saying, 'This year, we'll end up with a million in sales!' His company would always be expanding buildings," John said. "I remember that. What set them apart was how well they treated their employees. People working there wouldn't expect the large bonuses they would receive, either. They couldn't believe that much money would be coming to them. Some of the people who have been there 30 years, line workers, are now worth a lot in company stock."

Dick was not always devoted to giving, however. "When we were members of another church I was on the drive to collect pledges," Dick recalled. "I pledged $52 and every Sunday, I could put a dollar in the plate. If I had missed the previous week, I didn't put in two to make it up. The next year, I increased my pledge to $104, but found that nothing had changed; if I got behind, I emotionally couldn't make it up.

"One Sunday, a couple of men from that church came by our house to ask me if I would make up the $45 or $50 I was behind in the second year. I told them, 'No.' I have often wondered what they were thinking as they drove out of our drive and away from our nice house on 10 acres in Germantown. I know now that the ability to give is a grace from God — a grace I was not given until we started tithing."

The Bagbys were very impressed by Jinnie's business acumen. "Jinnie was an able manager and planner, though she rarely said such and such will either happen or not," John said. "Instead, she would contingency plan and it was not just a simple black and white proposition. She would try different things to make a situation or project work."

The couple also describe the Bodines as very religious in all tenets of the faith and regular Sunday School teachers.

"They had deep faith and relied on God and prayer to help them," John said. When they left Memphis many years later, the Bodines were part of reactivating a church on St. Croix. That was not a totally new endeavor to them after having helped start Faith Presbyterian while living in the Memphis area.

Their descriptions of Dick's and Jinnie's personalities are revealing: Neither would flaunt their wealth or intelligence, though both were very success-oriented, the said. Instead, they were known for getting along with the common man and making people feel like their equals.

It was all part of a journey, a constant unfolding discovery of faith and its meaning in life. Now, Dick and Peggy continue together in the walks of faith that each started in his or her own way years ago, accented by a lot of lessons from the Lord and from life.

X

The Bodine School

T HE BODINE SCHOOL, LIKE SOME OTHER charitable, health care and educational institutions in America, grew from the seeds of tragedy. Dick and Jinnie's son, Rick, had a strong IQ, but could not learn new materials easily. For two highly educated engineers, this was a new and different type of challenge. However, like everything else the Bodines dealt with, they handled the situation with understanding, research and creative problem-solving.

"When our son was accepted into the first grade at Presbyterian Day School, he scored over 140 on the IQ tests," Jinnie Bodine wrote in a 1993 letter. In spite of his intelligence, he struggled in school. It was not until the fourth grade that a child psychiatrist who had moved to Memphis from the Menninger Clinic in Kansas diagnosed him as having learning disabilities. There already had been diagnosis after diagnosis. The Bodines had tried everything.

The next year, two experimental classes were formed at Memphis State University. Rick was one of the 14 selected for these classes of 150 who applied. Local parents raised money to send two teachers to Dallas to be trained in this area. Rick made some minor progress, and, at the end of two years, he entered the seventh grade at a school in Germantown. Shortly thereafter, Rick was transferred to the slower-learner class, where he spent four long, miserable years failing.

The psychiatrist who diagnosed Rick told them about the Mills School in Ft. Lauderdale, Fla. At 15, Rick was accepted there, the nearest and best such school at the time for dyslexia. At that time, about 14 students from the Memphis area attended Mills then. Dick and Jinnie could not afford the tuition, so an aunt of Jinnie's, Ann Pagels, who was also a teacher, offered to pay the tuition.

"The school knew what to do and how to teach a child like this," Jinnie said. "It was like a miracle. At the end of the first year, he came home happy, eager and for the first time, talking about college." Much of Rick's frustrations were gone, too, and Dick said they didn't hear doors slamming or experience his temper tantrums. Rick even received the school award for the most progress in math. The next year at Mills, he was taking all senior subjects and was scheduled for the college entrance tests. But their joy would soon turn to deep sorrow.

Rick's class was swimming in the Atlantic Ocean for a school event and there was a buddy system in place. The ocean began to get rough, so they rang a bell for the students to get out. Rick's buddy said later that Rick had been close to him, but when everyone was out, Rick was missing. Life guards and helicopters searched and found his body much later near where he had last been seen. Adding to the puzzling side of the deep hurt is that Rick had been a good swimmer.

That night, Dick and Jinnie were working late at the company. Everyone had gone. The phone rang with the terrible message that Rick had drowned. To this day, Dick shies away from answering the phone. Jinnie would say in later years that this was the first thing she had not been able to get over, go around or through.

"Sometime later, we realized how many students from this area needed a school such as the Mills School," Dick said. Not too long afterward, the Bodines met with the same doctor who had diagnosed Rick and asked him how many children he had seen in

The Bodine School

a given year who had a similar learning disability and discovered there were some 30 new local cases annually which this doctor witnessed. After determining the need for local youngsters to have enriched learning through teachers skilled in working in the realm of learning disabilities, the Bodines established The Bodine School in 1972 as a private, nonprofit institution. The concept was to teach the students academic subjects and build their self-esteem at the same time.

Initially, the Bodines had considered the idea of establishing the school as an extension of the Mills School of Fort Lauderdale, with a campus name of the Mills School at Memphis. It subsequently became evident that the school would have to stand on its own, rather than becoming a branch of Mills. The Bodine School was created without Mills' financial backing. However, Dr. R.E. Mills, founder of the school by his name, visited the area several times, holding public meetings and working with the steering committee and the architect.

"I was naïve about building a school and that was probably a good thing," Dick said, for had he and Jinnie known what it would cost to run, they might not have had the nerve to do it. The couple started the school fairly close to the time they started the company. They were watching every penny. Therefore, they began the school before they had substantial funds to do so.

Based on the psychiatrist's estimate of students with this challenge, the Bodines assumed they would start with approximately 30 students. They hired eight teachers with a first-year budget of $130,000.

The school initially rented space from Frayser Presbyterian Church. When the doors opened for the first day of classes, it had just two students on the rolls, although a staff to serve 30 students. About four teachers were then laid off. Their contracts called for three months of employment initially. The Bodines didn't have the money to pay them but the Bodines promised the teachers they would be paid as soon as the Bodines had the money.

Several of the teachers went to the newspaper about the early episode. A reporter called Jinnie questioning her as though she had no intention of paying them. That writer pushed Jinnie beyond her limits and tried to put words in her mouth. Finally, Jinnie slammed the phone down.

Then a positive thing occurred when four more students came and the school stood on a little better footing – with some help.

"I had coffee in 1973 with a businessman whom I'd bought wire from and told him we were $5,000 short," Dick recalled. "He taught one of our students in Sunday School. He asked Jinnie and me to stop by his house one night. We did and I couldn't believe it, but he had a check with a five followed by three zeroes. I could not believe anyone was generous enough to give that amount. It saved the school the first year. Years later I told him, "You didn't know what you did then, but you saved the school."

When the need arose to move from their initial location, Dick was driving down Poplar Avenue and noticed the Kingsway Christian Church. The Lord led him to do something he hated to do and wasn't good at – making a cold call on someone. He asked for the pastor, who listened to Dick's story. They entered into an agreement that very day. The Bodine School moved there its second year and stayed at Kingsway until the Bodines could build on their own acreage on Dogwood Road in Germantown.

The couple set aside about half of their 10 acres on Dogwood for the school to further help it flourish and so that it could have its own site. With advice from the Mills School, they had buildings designed specifically for the learning disabled. The architect for the first building, Robert Thomas Martin, contributed his services and the building was completed in 1979. For years, Dick never knew where Jinnie found the money. When Dick asked Jinnie, she told him not to worry about it.

There were interesting interludes early on regarding things the Bodines had not previously known about their property once the school was built on their back acreage in Germantown. "One day, we walked to the south end of the (school) property and discovered the back end of it missing," Jinnie recalled in a letter many years later. "The subdivision development had begun and they had bulldozed off about 15 feet completely across to fill in the ditch so they could start building houses on it. They had to put it all back and sod it.

"The developer did fill in the ditch and install a concrete drain near the southeast corner of the school property and built houses over the ditch. The county accepted the development, probably without realizing that the drain was undersized," Jinnie wrote. A builder gave the school a 50-foot lot for access to the school property.

When it came time to build a new permanent building, before Dick knew it, a building "appeared" in 1979. Once again, Dick didn't know where the money had come from, but there are some indications that early funds came – at her request – from the estate of Anne Pagels, who had retired after teaching half a century in Beatrice, Neb., about 60 miles south of Lincoln. Miss Pagels was Rick's great aunt, and had followed his progress and that of the school's with enthusiasm. She also had been the person who had paid for Rick's tuition at the Mills School.

"We had a groundbreaking ceremony in dead winter and construction started. A ditch was dug along the south edge of the property for drainage," Jinnie wrote in her 1996 letter.

The early years of the school were fraught with some setbacks and drama. Funding problems developed early on. There was initial overhiring of some faculty without the student population to support it. Some contracts had to be cancelled. Early director William Sater was killed in an automobile accident. His successor, Roy Walker, later resigned because of ill health.

Then there were also successes. An autistic student started communicating and, over relatively rapid time, progressed from the second to ninth grade level. Another student won the Memphis Press Scimitar spelling bee. Yet another scored the highest ever in math on a college board exam – all during the second year of operation.

The ongoing mission of the The Bodine School continues to be to lead the Mid-South in teaching children with reading disabilities to read and to achieve success. The school helps students realize their individual learning needs while increasing their self-esteem, developing their creativity and improving their social interactions. In doing so, students are better able to select goals in life appropriate for their talents. The school is governed by a board of directors that meets six times a year and an executive committee that meets monthly.

The Bodine School Classrooms.

Someone with just a passing knowledge of dyslexia might think people with the learning disability perceive written letters differently than other individuals, but that is not the case. It is not a visually based disorder, said Dr. Rene Friemoth Lee, its current executive director, who has been the instrumental nucleus to the school's success since the month she arrived there in 1990. Rather, it involves a difficulty in connecting the sound of a word and that word in print. Dyslexia (derived from a Greek word meaning "difficulty with language") affects 15 percent of the population. The learning disability affects people of all intelligence and socio-economic levels. Most are creative out-of-the-box thinkers.

More specifically, this neurological disorder not only makes the acquisition of language skills difficult, it affects the ability to read, write, spell, speak or compute with normal proficiencies despite conventional instruction, a culturally adequate environment, proper motivation and normal intelligence. It is believed that dyslexia arises from a combination of physiological, neurological and genetic factors.

As research in learning disabilities progressed and programs were established, educators discovered that children learn quite differently from one another. Recognizing letters in the alphabet or numbers required these children to use their hands and sense of touch as well as their eyes. When a message from the eyes to the brain scrambled the letter "d" into a "b," their sense of touch had learned that "d" makes their fingers move to the left, and "b" to the right. Velvet, sandpaper, and other tactile materials formed into letters were used to start these students on the road to reading excellence. Patience, an emphasis on focus, and other teaching tools often allowed younger students to go on to regular public or private schools for high school, because they had learned ways to work around their particular learning problems.

Teachers at The Bodine School use a multisensory approach to reading. Parents of students there are also trained to work with their children at home. They are encouraged to read aloud to them because it helps them to learn. The goal at Bodine is for students to return to traditional schools. This school is designed for students who have average to very superior intellectual endowment, but who also have learning disabilities. It is not geared for those with lower intellectual ability with resulting learning problems.

In each course at the school, there is a balance among the activities to develop the cognitive, affective and psychomotor domains of instruction. Each student receives individual lessons, group lessons and special help, as needed. Students are led to remediate and compensate for their learning disabilities.

Germantown meanwhile annexed the area around the school. Jinnie later had a second building constructed that was adjacent and fully connected to the first one in addition to being very close in design. "When we built the north building, we found out about the undersized drain. Germantown told us we could not build another thing unless we put a pond at the southeast corner of the school property," Jinnie said. "The school exists because our son drowned during a physical education class at the Mills School. No way would we ever allow a pond on Bodine School property."

As for the other four acres toward Dogwood, Germantown gave the Bodines the option of building a wall or of grading from the house to street level. The latter meant that all the big old trees would be destroyed.

"Naturally, we chose the wall," Jinnie said. Germantown handled the specs and construction.

Some years later, the Bodines gave their house and the rest of their Germantown property to the school which sold it for some $400,000. The Bodines had bought the entire property for about $37,000 originally. The proceeds from the sale of the Bodine home property were placed in an endowment that is used to supplement teachers' salaries and to provide tuition assistance to families in need.

The 1980s saw several milestones: the school bought a van, tuition became more keyed to cost, the first African-American students enrolled, the Shelby County Board of Education contracted with the school, Dr. Mills continued to help set priorities and guidelines, the north building was built, and the school rented space to Faith Presbyterian Church to use on Sundays while their sanctuary was being built. The school also earned accreditation from the Southern Association of Colleges and Schools. In another alliance, The Bodine School and The University of Memphis have had a working relationship for 20-plus years. Each semester, U of M students who are special education majors meet their practicum requirements by observing for 30 hours at the school. The U of M students become involved in the classroom lessons and assist the lead teachers when possible. Similarly, other universities complete observation requirements at the school.

With an average 6-to-1 student-to-teacher ratio, the school is very expensive to operate. The Bodines continued to help subsidize part of its deficit.

"The Bodines have at the same time progressively backed away enough to let the school stand on its own feet," said Dr. Rene Lee. "This process began in about 1994 and it has been effective."

At this time, the school's leadership developed strict and formal job descriptions after the failure of several key hires. David Crippen became chairman of the board and Pearson Uhlhorn Crutcher began working as director of development. Together, they made several significant strides. Special projects, such as the library, science lab room and playground were funded by memorials and by the parent organization. The Virginia S. Bodine Library, dedicated in the year of her death, has stained wood shelves, a circulation desk, computer workstations and a story tower where students can relax and read. Funds raised to build and equip it came primarily from the 1999 Bodine School Auction and the Idita-Read program.

Pearson, now executive director of the Society of Entrepreneurs, worked as development director at the school from 1996 until 1999. During that time, the school celebrated several milestones, including its Silver Anniversary and also the Bodine's 50th wedding anniversary.

The first Community Leaders Breakfast also began during this period. The outreach brings in people who ordinarily would not know about the school and effectively showcases all of its programs. During Dyslexia Awareness Month, the school educates the public about its mission. The children invite the mayor, fire chief and other notable individuals to come to breakfast, and then tour the school to learn more about its mission and programs.

"It is a key way for the school to bring people in from the out-side and to let them see for themselves the unique features and what it offers the community," Pearson said.

The science lab, along with its many features, is a notable addition to the school. Four rectangular tables serve as experiment areas for the elementary students. The older students conduct lab experiments on three octagonal lab stations. The Assisi Foundation played an important role in funding the lab and underwriting for the tables, microscope case and tray table case. Related funds came from the ServiceMaster Company and The ServiceMaster Foundation. Students working in the lab have a set of high-tech microscopes. Ten student microscopes plus an instructor's microscope were purchased with a grant from The Medtronic Foundation. The Dorr Foundation in New York also awarded a grant to the school for the lab. The parent organization additionally contributed and raised money. None of its planning would have been possible without the talent and generosity of the late architect Lewis Ertz, father of Bodine Co.'s immediate past chief executive, Alex Ertz.

In similar fashion, the Technology Lab was set up in the 1990s with different organizations sponsoring each work station. "We started out with nine or 10 stations and it has grown from there," Pearson said.

The school's parent organizations raise money through events such as pansy sales and holiday wreath and poinsettia sales. The Midsouth Charity Air Show Foundation also has contributed proceeds to the school to help it fund academic and scholarship programs.

Initially, for several reasons the target student population was defined as those 12 years old and older. Public and other private schools were providing for the younger children, but help was not readily available for the older students. The reaching and teaching of 12, 14 or 16-year-old students who had failed for so many years is different from techniques used with younger children. In addition, older students must earn credits toward graduation. After some years, the school began to accept a few young students, but it was not until 1990 that classes were opened specifically for elementary-age students.

Although The Bodine School achieved state accreditation after two years, the Bodines' ultimate goal, which was reached the year they retired from the company, was for it to become accredited by the Southern Association of Colleges and Schools. When there was a high school component, it was not unusual for the school to have a 100 percent pass rate for all three state achievement tests for high school students with at least a third of the students scoring at the advanced level.

Since 2005, the school now averages between 80 and 90 students across grades one through eight. School leaders had decided to discontinue the high school program in order for the elementary program to grow, Rene said. This decision came at a time when there was earlier identification of learning disabilities, specifically dyslexia occurring more frequently among children.

The campus still is situated on a section of the Bodine's original property on Dogwood, but the revisions to the campus master plan show it is outgrowing its site.

In addition, Dick still provides occasional advising to assist the school in continuing to offer a unique educational opportunity for students with dyslexia.

"Truly, the history of this school is a testimony of continued acts of faith," Rene said. "It is the very definition of perseverance. There were numerous barriers in the early years. In spite of that, the Bodines and staff remained committed and do to this day."

In a tribute letter for Dick's 80th birthday, Rene wrote, "You have been a beacon in my life. When I think of generosity, I think of you. When I think of selflessness, I think of you. When I think of quiet strength, I think of you. When I think of faith, I think of you. Many times, when I became discouraged, your example kept me focused on the goal of helping students."

Through the years, a strong connection has existed between the company and the school, both in terms of financial and advisory support. David Crippen, Alex Ertz, Lamar Brock and others of the Bodine Co. have served on the The Bodine School's board of directors.

"The school's board of directors has the utmost respect for the Bodines," Rene said. "They revered them for their absolute unfailing faith and generosity for creating this school for others' children. We take that very seriously and want to maintain that commitment. It's not about the bottom line. It's about the child. The Bodines' legacy of community service and generosity continues here and at the company. We do our best to preserve that. We want to make sure we enable any child who needs to learn skills to go back into the community as a productive member."

Truly, early detection and intervention in children who display learning difficulties in acquiring reading skills are vital and can have a great impact on a child's success in school and in life. Poor readers, unless they receive strategic interventions in reading, fare poorly in the educational system and subsequently, the occupational ladder.

"What Jinnie and Dick created is so amazing and a true testimony of their yearning to give back to the community," Pearson said. "The growth and development that I saw in those students in the period I was there is almost indescribable in terms of its impact. I think Rene Lee is incredible. If it were not for the generosity of the Bodines, the school would not be there, but Dr. Lee's ongoing leadership is central and essential too. When you see kids getting the assistance they need and then getting them back into the schools that will serve them, you realize part of the true impact and opportunity it provides."

Several testimonial letters have come to the school over the years. Some epitomize its legacy. An excerpt of one letter attests, "The Bodine School has made such a difference in our lives. We have climbed out of that dark place into the light." And another states, "The Bodine School has been a true blessing for our son in his regained spirit, interest in learning and the experience of success."

For these reasons and more, countless other Mid-South area parents, students and alumni say, "Thank God for The Bodine School!"

TESTIMONIAL VIGNETTES

Alex Finke

ALEX FINKE'S STORY ISN'T ONE OF A SERIOUS ISSUE that suddenly came to the surface, rather a subtle rumble that gains strength over time. Without intervention, his would be an entirely different story.

Alex's reading ability seemed normal in the early childhood years. It was not until the family made a move from Texas to Tennessee half-way through his kindergarten year that his parents realized "he wasn't getting it." They attributed his difficulty in school to the move and to his exposure to an entirely different curriculum and reading program. However, by the second half of first grade, it became clear that Alex had a reading problem. Although his grades were acceptable, it was apparent he was struggling with learning how to read.

Following the usual battery of tests, it was determined that Alex had difficulty with phonemic awareness. At that time, it was suggested that a learning program such as the one at The Bodine School could help him. His parents, CJ and Ray Finke, consulted with his teachers at his school where he was then enrolled. Rather than taking the route of changing schools, they decided to pursue remediation. An IEP (Individualized Education Plan) was developed and followed. At the end of second grade, Alex was privately tested and the family learned he had not improved sufficiently in his test scores and was a full grade level behind in reading.

There were several factors that pushed his parents to make a change. Alex felt completely overwhelmed by the quantity of work required and was embarrassed when his third grade teacher asked him in front of the class why he was so slow in transcribing work from the board. It became obvious that he needed to be attending The Bodine School where his potential could be cultivated, rather than his self esteem being chipped away.

The pressure Alex was placing on himself was considerable and it was clearly time for intervention. His parents knew what needed to be done, but they didn't know how their son would react. When they told him about Bodine, his only reaction was "I want to go to a school where everyone is just like me."

Throughout those years before Alex enrolled at Bodine, the family went through the natural frustrations many parents of learning disabled students face: sensing that something was wrong, denying that a problem exists, relying on educators' assurance that all would be OK, tutoring and thinking the reading problem would get better with maturity.

Finally, at The Bodine School, the family became armed with information to serve as an advocate for their son.

Alex has since seen amazing changes over the years and has become a confident young man who is more resilient and determined. His work ethic and desire to succeed have truly been cultivated at Bodine School.

Karly Coleman

KARLY COLEMAN WAS ALWAYS THE LIFE OF THE party. Almost from the time she could speak, she'd light up a room. She never met a stranger and people seemed to be drawn to her. She was happy and well adjusted. Karly reached her milestones in a timely manner and everything seemed just fine.

Then one day, it was time for Karly to start school. Things seemed fine for Karly until she entered her 4-year-old preschool, her parents, Angie and Jason Coleman, recalled. They were told by her teachers that she was hiding under the table and disrupting the class. She didn't follow directions or seem to be listening. This didn't seem like their little girl at all. Could they have their children mixed up? Karly wasn't hyperactive and her hearing tests were fine. What was wrong?

Karly clearly could not focus in school, so her parents had her tutored in preschool to learn her letters and numbers. Then she started crying every time she was dropped off at school and did not want to go. She was a different child – but only at school.

After preschool ended, Jason and Angie decided to send their daughter to a small private kindergarten. They hoped that this environment would provide what she needed. But Karly had a very difficult time in kindergarten. She struggled to pay attention and to keep up with the rest of the class.

Her parents had to get help, but didn't know where. They had more questions than answers and tried several options to find Karly the help that she needed; however, nothing was working.

The Colemans were familiar with The Bodine School because they had attended a silent auction for several years with their friends. They enjoyed the auctions and thought highly of the school. After attending the auction in 2003, they decided to call

The Bodine School to see if they could help Karly. That phone call put them on the right track. While they still had no idea that Karly had dyslexia, they just knew they were headed in the right direction.

After Karly was diagnosed with dyslexia, the Colemans still had much work to do. The family was referred to another reading-based learning program for more extensive remediation. After five months in the program, they were ready for The Bodine School. Karly was accepted there in 2004. Now, Karly has regained her confidence and has thrived there. She is much happier and enjoys school. It has not been easy for her and many tasks are still somewhat difficult. However, the school has given and continues to give her the tools to help her to be successful in the future, no matter where she is. She definitely doesn't hide under the table at school anymore.

Steven Joe

STEVEN JOE IS THE YOUNGEST OF THREE CHILDREN.
Ever since he was born, his parents Penn and Clara Joe have
known he was learning in a different kind of way, although he
liked to explore life to the fullest. His ability to reason and to
think outside the box is both amusing and amazing.

He would constantly create objects from ordinary household
items. The combination of his artistic and moral compasses made
him think that it was his obligation, for instance, to tell his teen-
age sister just what he considered to be fashionable. He did this,
though with a heart of compassion and generosity.

Beginning at age four, Steven had shown signs of a slight speech
delay. The onset of speech therapy also marked the beginning of
an emotional roller coaster into the world of learning disabilities.
In preschool, Steven had difficulty mastering shapes and colors.
By the end of preschool, he still did not remember his address,
phone number or days of the week.

They then decided to send Steven to a Montessori school for
kindergarten. He was excited about school and wanted to learn.
Toward the conclusion of the fall semester, it was evident that his
spirit was slowly changing. He didn't talk about what he did in
school anymore.

Initially, homework consisted of printing alphabet letters. Steven's attempt at print was as arduous as his attempt at pencil grip-
ping, which his parents attributed to his being left-handed. Steven also had an inclination to write his letters backward. More
often than not, his name was written backward and inverted.

He brought home beginner's phonetic booklets to practice
reading at home. The first few books seemed easy for him. How-

ever, the progression of booklets revealed the disparity between his ability to read and the school's expectations.

Steven's parents even talked to his teachers several times throughout the year about his multiple difficulties, but were repeatedly told he did not exhibit any problems at school. Even in a Montessori setting, he was innately aware that he just could not write and read like his peers. He didn't understand why, although he tried very hard. He felt bad about himself, his parents said, and he often wanted to stay home.

By age five, he learned to fear school. Homework became a battle and Steven's personality changed from being carefree to insecure. Home was no longer a respite from school.

Steven was tested at the end of his kindergarten year. Upon receiving the "reading disorder" diagnosis, the family was relieved and thankful because they knew there was a school in Memphis just for children like their son.

The family had heard Dr. Lee speak at a library several years ago about how children learn how to read. Teaching a dyslexic child to read is difficult, but there are scientifically-based methodologies proven to ensure success.

Steven entered The Bodine School in 2002. Meetings with Dr. Lee and his first grade teacher were a major contrast to the family's past experiences. They met to discuss educational plans individualized to Steven and respectful to his differences. Because of his early scholastic failures, Steven had learned to hide his vulnerabilities of being angry and defiant, even at school. His first grade teacher and Dr. Lee understood him and allowed his outbursts. Steven learned to accept himself, and thus, regained self-esteem and developed academic confidence. His healing began at The Bodine School.

Steven transitioned out of the school after the fourth grade. He entered a mainstream Christian private school where he received support services such as typed class notes, study guides and extended time during tests. He adapted quickly to the new school environment and made many friends. In fifth grade, he made all As and one B. Steven turned 12 in 2008 and finished sixth grade with all As and one B. He was placed in honors math in seventh grade. The gift of The Bodine School resonates in Steven's academic achievements and his love for reading. It has clearly done so for so many others, as well.

XI

Parallel Lives and New Phases of Change: St. Croix and Memphis

ICK'S LIFE TODAY IS MUCH CHANGED, AS anyone's would be after living more than 80 years, fighting in a world war, starting and running a successful company and losing the wife of his youth. However, life with wife, Peggy, has so many pleasant connecting points with their mutual past. After the couple met, they discovered how many things they had in common over the years.

"I also knew the Jemison family well over the years and after Dick and Peggy got to know each other, it was evident to me how much the Jemison family really embraced Dick," friend Herbert Rhea said. "It has been wonderful for him and for Peggy."

As a historian, Peggy encouraged the recording of Dick's life and, as such, also served as the initiator to have the history of both the school and company encompassed in this volume. Peggy brought Dick a sizeable family, three married children and eight grandchildren, along with companionship and love in his senior years.

Peggy and Dick had lived parallel lives in some respects, something that only became evident later. They were both born in Memphis at Methodist Hospital – and just six months apart. They had grown up with many of the same friends and both had

Dick and Peggy Bodine.

attended Miss Freda's dancing class, though they didn't know each other then.

Before Peggy met Dick, she attended Wheaton College and then returned to Memphis with the intention of transferring to Southwestern at Memphis, now Rhodes College. Then the war ended and she met Frank Jemison, an aeronautical engineer who had worked on airplanes first at Langley Field, Va., and then he was employed at Fischer Body Works in Memphis. His father, W.D. Jemison, who had a real estate business, enlarged the company to be W.D. Jemison & Sons with the addition of both sons, Bill and Frank. Peggy and Frank were married in 1947, a year after Jinnie and Dick married.

Frank Jr. was born in 1948. Meanwhile, Frank and Peggy congratulated each other that they were born in Memphis and would always live there. However, the company received a very large contract to build 450 houses at Tyndall Air Force Base in Panama City, Fla. Congress had voted in the Wherry Bill, which was a means of building houses for the services in league with private companies. The Jemisons moved to Panama City while Frank built the project and organized its rentals. They lived there the next two and a half years, coming back to Memphis in about 1953. Homebuilding was on the rise in Memphis and the Jemisons were involved in that activity. About that time, a good friend and future hotel magnate, Kemmons Wilson, invited some homebuilders to his house to tell them of his idea for a new kind of motel. The Jemisons bought franchises for several locations, becoming early investors in Holiday Inn.

Peggy and Frank had two more children, Marguerite (Meg), born in 1954, and Marshall, who was born two years later. They lived on Audubon Drive and participated in church, civic and educational activities in the Memphis community.

After Peggy completed her undergraduate studies at Wheaton, she placed family life at the forefront and permitted it to interrupt her academic pursuits for some years, realizing that she could return to formal studies at the right juncture. By the early 1960s, she returned to school, this time to then Memphis State University and completed her B.A. degree in English in 1965.

"I took several stops here and there for the welcome interruptions of marriage and motherhood and I wouldn't have done it any other way," Peggy said. "I encourage today's young people to allow themselves the freedom to make stops and embrace unexpected turns in their educational lives. Sometimes, the most unexpected things bring about the greatest blessings."

In 1969, Peggy returned to Memphis State, taking a couple of courses each year. A longtime interest in historical preservation and her minor studies in history prompted her to return to school to pursue a master's degree. Over the next years, while raising her family and leading an active civic and church life, she earned her master's degree in history in 1974. Later in 1992, she would obtain a doctorate in history.

All was going well for the Jemison family until Frank Sr.'s health began to fail. By 1980, they had decided to sell their family home and move into the Country Club Tower condominiums that Kemmons Wilson was completing in Memphis. By 1981, Frank had been diagnosed with a pituitary gland tumor which was removed in January of that year. In the ensuing years, his health and business declined. .

Years later, Dick and Jinnie moved in next door to them on the 10th floor of the same building. The couples had known each other casually, Peggy said. "The Bodines had retired and built a home in St. Croix and were in the process of giving their home on Dogwood to the Bodine School, but they still wanted to keep a place in Memphis," she recalled. "So for the next few years, we were neighbors in the building. When they would come to Memphis, we would see them for a few visits now and then."

Peggy and Dick Bodine in St. Croix.

Then Frank and Jinnie each began to experience severe health problems. Frank had a massive stroke from which he never recovered. He died in 1999. Jinnie developed breast cancer, for which she had operations and chemotherapy, enjoying some periods of remission. Jinnie also died in that same year. Both the Jemisons and the Bodines had long and successful marriages, the Jemisons for 52 years and the Bodines for 53.

Now alone, Dick and Peggy grew steadily in friendship and in love. In March 2000, they were married in the chapel of Second Presbyterian Church with a reception at the home of her son, Frank and his wife, Jeanne Jemison. Both Dick and Peggy sensed that God had brought them together to share their lives with each other, and so they have. This marriage also brought Dick a large and loving family. A grandson, Marshall Bodine Jemison, called "Bo," even shares his name. His parents, Marshall and Hilda Jemison, live in Chattanooga with another son, King.

Daughter-in-law Jeanne Jemison paid this tribute to Dick at his 80th birthday celebration. "I admire your humility and lack of self-promotion in spite of your remarkable and extraordinary accomplishments. I think of your leading by example and the legacy you have left with the Bodine Co. every time I hear of another community service or support they have provided. The quality of the endeavors you have devoted your abilities and involvement to reflect the high level of your own integrity and interests." Frank Jemison Jr., with their children, Elizabeth, Frank III and Sarah, join her in their appreciation of Dick.

Dick and Peggy lived for years in St. Croix, Virgin Islands, but in 2008 made the decision to consolidate residences back in Memphis because of the logistics of keeping up two homes so far apart, the advanced healthcare in Memphis and the desire to be closer to family. Still, the individual and collective legacies of Dick, Jinnie, and Peggy will never be forgotten on St. Croix.

The Bodine Visitor Center, part of the larger St. George Village Botanical Garden, serves as a permanent monument to their contributions to the island. Dick and Jinnie agreed to build a new visitor center, a plan which was presented to them when she was alive. Due to a change in the design and cost of the building, as well as new voices on the board of governors, ground was not broken until July 2001. Jinnie was now dead, so it was the pleasure of Dick and Peggy to complete this project. The beautiful Visitor Center Museum and store were formally opened in March 2006 and dedicated in loving memory to Virginia Shannon Bodine.

Today, the lush center features thousands of internationally known and endangered plants found only in the Caribbean. The

The Bodine Visitor Center, part of the larger
St. George Village Botanical Garden.

courtyard is the focus of activities and the Great Hall is available for weddings and other island events. Hortensia of Chalgub-Lanio Architects donated half of her architectural fees for the development of the documents for the Visitor Center construction. The architect wanted the center to evoke the feeling of a small village with buildings tied together with galleries. It can accommodate large tour groups in the pavilion, where information panels describe the garden and its attractions.

Where did the spark for this kind of devotion emanate? During his trips throughout the Caribbean, Dick had visited botanical gardens, each proclaiming itself to be the best. Those visits together inspired him to improve the one in St. Croix. "Now, none of them can touch the quality of this one," Dick said. "We were glad to help St. Croix."

Dedication.

Not all has been a sedentary life on the island, though. There were more exciting and adventurous times mixed in with the bucolic pastimes.

Retired Air Force Colonel Lou Harris, a longtime friend who met the Bodines through golfing circles, recalls a time when a side-swiping hurricane had blown the Bodine's 12-foot satellite antenna away in the mid-1990s, and he found it three or four days later down the mountain from the house in a deep ravine. Lou went to help Dick retrieve the power arm and the head. After taking a look at their location, Lou went home and returned with a considerable amount of rope. The side of the ravine was so steep that they had to tie ropes to the trees to have something to hold onto as they lowered themselves down to the antenna. The drop must have been 200 feet, Lou said, and going down was fairly easy. The antenna was stuck in the top of a tree, and Dick was able to climb on top of it and recover the equipment. Lou, meanwhile, was underneath taking the power arm off. With that done, they started to crawl out and what a climb that was, Lou recalled.

"I will never forget how winded and tired we were upon reaching the top and our falling to the ground to recover," he said. "It's a wonder that two 70-year-old men didn't die of heart attacks then and there."

Another time, the two worked hard to repair Dick's gate opener, taking a long time for Dick to develop and draw an electrical schematic, only to turn the cover over and discover the schematic on the inside.

The Bodine Visitor Center in the St. George Village Botanical Garden.

Time after time, there are testimonies of a stubborn Dick not wanting to buy off-the-shelf solutions to electronic needs. Alex recalls another such story. Dick would spend months at St. Croix and return to Memphis only to find that the backup system for his Lexus battery would be dead because of the long intervals. Rather than buying a trickle charger, he asked Alex to build him one. In Dick's way of thinking, buying one wouldn't be nearly as fun as making one.

Yet another time, Lou and Dick hauled diesel fuel after the hurricanes to power the Bodines' generator and needed power of another kind when they had a flat tire on the way.

It was during one of these hurricanes, namely Hurricane Hugo, that Dick's and Jinnie's allegiance toward the island and its people came into play again. When nobody else was investing, they believed so strongly in the Carambola development where they lived that they bought additional land on Prosperity Ridge to help ensure the success of their community, recalled Wendy Jacobs Ramos, landscape architect and former president of the garden. She advanced the development of the visitor center.

"Although our hospital suffered with shrinking budgets, Dick and Jinnie had faith in the hardworking doctors and nurses at the hospital – enough faith to quietly provide support for equipment they so desperately needed," Wendy added. "And when their church congregation was looking for a new home so it could grow to serve the community, they supported their Christian faith and quietly and generously provided support for the construction of the new multipurpose building and school."

Grand-daughter May Leinhart, daughter of Meg and Mike Bartlett, sums it up well when she speaks of Dick's "lovable humility and humorous unwillingness to take yourself too seriously." She added that Dick has a light touch, yet is such a bright light, a fixed point of strength for all of those around him. Her brothers, Jemison and Marshall Bartlett, agree.

The St. Croix chapter of the Bodines' lives, meanwhile began to change during 2008, when Dick and Peggy decided to place their island home on the market. Their desire to do so, although they were initially somewhat ambivalent, soon was confirmed as a sound decision via a newfound confidence in seeing a solid buyer come forward when the home was listed.

Award-winning national broadcast journalist and book author Bonnie Anderson bought the Bodines' scenic home at St. Croix, named "Oh Wow" because of the view. Bonnie, an outstanding journalist, worked at NBC and CNN over 27 years and was nominated for a Pulitzer and was awarded several Emmy Awards for her reporting. "It gives us a wonderful feeling knowing the interesting background of the person who bought our home," said Peggy.

The entrance to the house in St. Croix that Jinnie named "Oh Wow!"

Appropriately, Dick and Peggy now have returned to live out their lives in Memphis where so much of their history started. Here, they will write a new chapter in their lives and, if the past is any reflection of the future, they have more exciting times in store. They will also continue to touch and to influence many others whose lives intersect with theirs. Such has been, and continues to be the story of the Bodines, the company and the school.

Appendix

Year	Major Events with the Jemisons, Bodines, and the Company	Major Events with the School
1942	Dick enters World War II	
1946	Dick and Jinnie marry	
1946	Dick receives honorable discharge from U.S. Army	
1947	Frank and Peggy Jemison marry	
1950	Dick graduates from Georgia Tech	
1952	Rick Bodine is born	
1962	Bodine Company is founded	
1964	*Tran*-BAL® invented	
1965	Request comes in for lighted ad panels on taxi cabs	
1967	Company opens first plant in Collierville.	
1969	The untimely death of Rick Bodine	
1972		Bodine School is established
		School is admitted to membership in the National Association of Private Schools for Exceptional Children
1977		Two students are graduated; groundbreaking ceremony for first building

Year	Major Events with the Jemisons, Bodines, and the Company	Major Events with the School
1979		First permanent campus school building is completed; first yearbook is published
1980	Dick's heart bypass surgery	
1982	Wire supply company is purchased	
1984	Employee stock owner- ship plan is created	
1984	Company is selected Small Busi- ness of the Year for 1983 during a Memphis Business Journal cer- emony attended by 1,000 people	The North Building is constructed and opened
1988	Dick and Jinnie Bodine retire and finalize the sale of the company to the employees and move to the Virgin Islands.	Bodine School is accredited by the Southern Association of Schools and Colleges
1990		Dr. Rene Friemoth Lee accepts the position as new director
1999	Jinnie Bodine dies	
1999	Frank Jemison Sr. dies	
2000	Dick and Peggy marry	
2006	Philips Electronics of the Netherlands acquire the Bodine Co.	
2008		The Bodines return home to Memphis to live